THE ENTREPRENEUR'S FRAMEWORK

HOW BUSINESSES ARE *Adapting* IN THE NEW ECONOMY!

the *Entrepreneur's* FRAMEWORK

JOSHUA H. DAVIDSON

LIONCREST
PUBLISHING

THE ENTREPRENEUR'S FRAMEWORK

How Businesses Are Adapting in the New Economy

ISBN   978-1-5445-1264-8 *Paperback*

       978-1-5445-1263-1 *Ebook*

CONTENTS

PROLOGUE

It is essential that I am completely honest with you: *I wrote this book for myself.*

I wrote it for the person I was back in 2009, a mostly clueless sixteen-year-old who became an entrepreneur quite by accident.

I wrote it for myself today, as I continue to face the everyday obstacles, emotional battles, major defeats, and occasional small victories that come with being an entrepreneur.

I wrote it for my future self, so I will always have a reminder of exactly why I do what I do, then and now.

Writing this book is not for my own personal financial gain or ego. Trust me, there are far more effective ways to make money and boost the ego than writing a book. After spending more than three years of my life painstakingly rewriting multiple drafts of this book, I would go as far as saying writing this book has been a highly *unprofitable* venture.

However, I have always been and will remain a passionate student of entrepreneurship, and I still have many questions left to answer. The biggest one is: how can I continuously keep myself grounded through the endless challenges and obstacles that have yet to occur? I hope by the time that not-so-distant future arrives, I will have all the answers, or at least most of them.

That's another reason why I wrote this book—to continue providing myself with the context, perspective, and tools necessary for what it takes to be successful in this game called entrepreneurship, and to remind myself of the daily effort and mental fortitude that is necessary to keep it all going. I want this to be the book that reminds me, every day, just how damn special being an entrepreneur is, and how grateful I am to have this luxury, this lifestyle, and this responsibility. I want this book to be a beacon of light during the rough times that surely will come again. I need it as a counterweight to keep me grounded during the rocky times ahead.

I want this book to accomplish the same for you, too. I want it to be *even more* than that for you. Yes, I might have written this book for myself, but I know others share the same pains and hardships as I have, and will find value in this.

This book is meant for anyone who is like me, wants to become me, and will surpass me. I hope to pass my knowledge and experiences on to you, and by doing so, inspire you to dive headfirst into the world of entrepreneurship if you haven't already.

While some may claim that the path to becoming a successful entrepreneur is not easily quantifiable, I've learned to live by a few key principles. This is a framework that has taken me more than a decade to recognize and appreciate. It's one that I need to remind myself about often, and want to teach you.

This set of principles acts as my compass. The further away I drift from these principles, the more likely I will lose, I will burn out, and I won't be the lasting entrepreneur I envision myself to be or will become.

I'VE SEEN HUNDREDS OF ENTREPRENEURS QUIT THIS GAME

For most people, it just doesn't work out.

Nine out of every ten startups will fail in the first five years. While some can weather the storm of constant stress and turmoil, more often than not, they simply cannot withstand the impact when sky-high expectations crash into reality.

Sometimes this failure is due to entrepreneurs acting as their own worst enemies, while other times it's due to factors simply out of their control. Some people whom I have considered to be the most intelligent, hardworking individuals I've ever met had to quit entrepreneurship because they just weren't cut out for this game.

But why?

I needed to understand how these talented, driven, and intelligent people could fail at entrepreneurship, while someone like me—a random kid from Egg Harbor Township, New Jersey, with no entrepreneurial influences and blessed with only a fraction of those other individuals' natural talents and intelligence—could be considered successful in this game.

Why was I not part of that 90 percent who fail within the first five years of building their own business? During my darkest moments (some of which took place even as I wrote this book), why didn't I quit like just about everyone else? What could possibly separate me and the other 10 percent from all the rest?

These are questions that have captivated me and that I

knew over the years I needed to research, observe, and ultimately discover.

I'VE HAD TO CAREFULLY DEFINE AND CONSTRUCT THIS FRAMEWORK THROUGH YEARS OF TRIAL AND ERROR

Some of you who are reading this book may have already known about me. You might even think of me as a success, given the following:

- You hear that I've been an entrepreneur for a decade, working on my company, Chop Dawg.
- You see that I've helped build and launch more than 250 web, mobile, and wearable apps.
- You've seen that I've worked with some of the largest brands and *Fortune* 500s in the world.
- You hear that I employ dozens of people.
- You hear that I work with clients all across the globe.
- You see that I travel the world, speaking at events, conferences, universities, and seminars.
- You see that I have hundreds of thousands of fans on social media.
- You've seen newspaper articles, magazine articles, podcast interviews, radio interviews, blog posts, and so on, about me.
- You've heard me host on the radio and on podcasts about entrepreneurship.
- You even see that I am (now) a published author.

This is what I consider the *highlight reel.*

It's accurate, but it doesn't speak at all to the hundreds of failures that it took to eventually get to the steady success that I (mostly) enjoy today. It doesn't include the internal battles, the close-to-the-brink legal troubles, or the fights with team members, clients, vendors, and partners. It doesn't show the nights when my mind was *my* own worst enemy or the days when I wondered if I was going to be able to make payroll or find that next client, and felt almost paralyzed due to the fear of becoming an embarrassment to those whom I look up to most. It doesn't show the moments when I felt so frustrated, so angered, that I would turn into the Incredible Hulk. And it certainly doesn't cover those sudden, unexpected moments that have derailed entire plans that my team and I spent months (and sometime years) researching, investing, and planning...all to just fail spectacularly.

Yes, my business belongs to the 10 percent success rate, those elusive businesses that were able to make it past the first five years. But I still feel it's so important for me to show that I've had more failures than successes on my journey. I refuse to glamorize entrepreneurship or bullshit my own story. I owe it to you to be candid and direct throughout every single page of this journey you are about to embark on. I am not a top entrepreneur, and I'm nowhere near the class of some of the tech giants you read about and watch every day. However, I've managed to do something that *most* in this game fail at: build a business that is viable, provides real value, makes real money, solves real problems, is bigger than myself, and is self-sufficient.

Entrepreneurship is naturally cutthroat. It is emotionally draining. It will take everything out of you, and it has no obligation to give anything back. It will challenge you in ways you cannot fathom. This is why you must understand not only the strategies necessary for playing this game but also understand how the game is played.

And the scariest part? *You need to fear becoming complacent and taking things for granted. You need to use your natural fear of being an entrepreneur and turn it into an endless source of motivation to be better.*

There is a popular saying in stoicism: *memento mori,* which in Latin means "remember that you have to die." It can feel morbid and frightening to consider your own death, but to me, *memento mori* reminds me to not take a single day, action, or interaction for granted. We all have a very limited time on this planet to do something that counts. It is the single biggest factor to why I've spent a decade crafting the framework you see below.

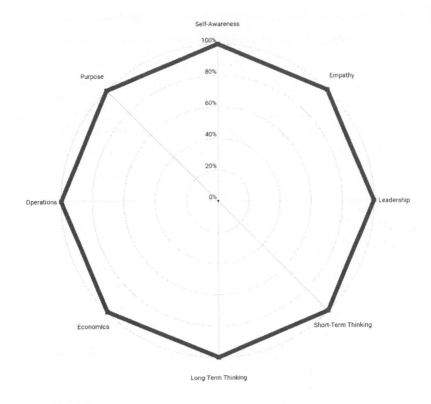

I've also come to adapt to the rules and take advantage of some of the perks of the New Economy that we'll dive into more throughout this book:

1. There has never been a greater number of things that you can try with the tools that are now available. It has never been more affordable or faster to start a new business, too.

2. This abundance of digital resources also makes the pool of entrepreneurs bigger than ever before.

3. Data are the new oil; they're the resource that is being extracted from people's heads. However, data in themselves are intrinsically worthless. It's *how* you can turn them into money that makes them a worthwhile resource.

4. Humanity is on the cusp of changing the world, and a new species will arise with artificial intelligence (AI). Business will become decentralized, smarter, and more efficient in ways we can't even imagine in the present moment.

5. Even with everything that is new, there are fundamentals of the economy that stay the same through time, foundational blocks that the New Economy won't ever change.

Once you've thoroughly learned this framework, you'll also be able to identify all of the principles in other successful entrepreneurs. Even if they don't recognize the very framework that they themselves are using, *you'll* be able to see how they applied the logic to their endeavors, investments, and daily behaviors. This has been one of the greatest, most remarkable things I've uncovered as I learned this framework myself.

Whether you're a first-time entrepreneur, serial entrepreneur, struggling entrepreneur, hobbyist-turned-entrepreneur, small-business-minded or *Fortune* 500-minded, tech- or brick-and-mortar-based—whatever you might be—I hope this book provides you with the values, insights, motivations, and knowledge that you need while you're on your entrepreneurial journey.

Thank you for reading, and please do enjoy *The Entrepreneur's Framework: How Businesses Are Adapting in the New Economy.*

—

From the very beginning of this journey to create *The Entrepreneur's Framework*, I decided that any profits generated from its sales would be donated to Big Brothers Big Sisters (Independence Region). Based in my home city of Philadelphia, Pennsylvania, this is a cause that I care deeply about and an organization for which I personally volunteer and give back to.

In this ever-changing world, it is more important than ever for us to nurture mentorship in our youth to ensure a better and brighter tomorrow.

Section 1

WHY

CHAPTER 1

WHY YOU NEED A FRAMEWORK

Let's say you want to get good at basketball. You decide to head out to the courts and get in some practice on your free throws and lay-ups. While mastering those moves may be what initially appeals to you the most, it's not *the very first thing you need to work on.*

No, the first thing that you actually need to learn is how the sport of basketball works. You need to build up your basketball IQ. You'll never get good at free throws and lay-ups until you understand the fundamental events in the game that lead to them.

However, even after mastering the fundamentals, you don't jump right into free throws and lay-ups. *Not yet.*

What you should do is start focusing on the essentials of the game, the most straightforward mechanisms that allow you to play the sport: dribbling, passing, proper shooting techniques. You continue to practice these daily, every minute on the minute, until eventually, they become second nature to you.

You apply this same strategy to the moves that originally attracted you to the sport—yes, your free throws and lay-ups—while learning and perfecting the complex pieces of the game.

Sure, lay-ups and free throws are what initially interested you. But by this point, if you're still in the game, it is because you've caught the bug. You want to become better. You want to join a team and actually compete against others. You've only just begun the journey to learning how to play basketball. Now that you've learned the fundamentals of the game, *you can begin to understand how to become masterful at the game, and therefore how to win.* The lay-ups and the free throws are now in your bag of tools.

Entrepreneurship is no different. I've seen countless first-time entrepreneurs jump into this game without first taking the time to learn how the game works. I've also seen entrepreneurs who have, against all odds, seen short-term success but failed to grow or last because they never took the time to educate themselves on the rules of this game.

I've also seen too many entrepreneurs quickly become complacent with the tools at their disposal, without ever taking the time to learn how to connect those tools to a bigger strategy. Once they found a formula they were comfortable with, they never discovered the new ways they could play the game.

Masterful basketball players think of the game more like a chess match than just an athletic contest between two different teams. If you want to be the best on the court, you learn about defensive and offensive strategies, what a 1-3-1 formation is, which position is responsible for what, when to foul, when not to foul, proper usage of time-outs, the history of the sport...the list goes on and on.

You also learn about yourself as a player. You fine-tune your fitness, your meals, your macronutrients, and your sleeping patterns, all to give yourself that competitive advantage.

You continue to learn and practice. You continue to train, trying to find that edge. You watch tapes of your competition, trying to find weaknesses to exploit.

Over time, you start to realize that you're not the only one who's hungry. Your teammates, your coaches, and your competitors all feel the same, work the same, and focus on the same. You use this as motivation to work even harder, faster, better.

Not everyone can be a professional basketball player. There are certain things you cannot build, such as athleticism, size, and natural, raw talent.

Entrepreneurship, for better or for worse, doesn't create such a physical barrier for inclusion. This creates the illusion that anyone with a good idea can make it in this game. But there *is* a reason why so few of them do.

I HAVE BROKEN THIS BOOK INTO TWO DISTINCT PARTS, THE WHY AND HOW

There are thousands of individuals out there who shoot tremendous free throws or make decent lay-ups time after time. But you don't see them playing professional basketball, do you? It takes so much more than just being good at one small part of a complex game. It requires a holistic understanding of all of the parts of the game that you're playing and how to put them all together to be successful.

The same is true if you want to win big in entrepreneurship. You need to learn the fundamentals, the strategies, and the rules of navigating through the New Economy. Once you have that understanding, you can *then* start practicing the plays.

You also, perhaps most importantly, need to learn the why in yourself. What I mean about the why is, what are you doing besides being an entrepreneur? Entrepreneurs who have found their why will not tell you that their chief motivation is "entrepreneurship" or "making money." They may tell you that they want to provide clean drinking water to people who didn't previously have access. They may tell you that they started a YouTube channel to educate people on their finances, to help others avoid making the financial mistakes they once made themselves. Your why is whatever mission you want to fulfill, and if you need to start it yourself, entrepreneurship is the vehicle to get there.

Once you understand the why, you'll be able to understand the how. This is where you begin diving deeper into more complex, advanced strategies in order to win the game. You'll learn how it relates to all of the following pieces that make up the framework throughout this book: *self-awareness, empathy, leadership, short-term and long-term thinking, economics, operations,* and *purpose.*

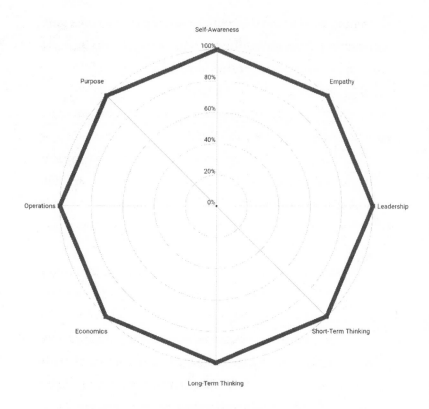

This is the framework that you'll begin to soon understand, adapt, and leverage. Soon, I will walk you through how to use the framework and the visual spider chart that is used throughout this book.

IN A LOT OF WAYS, THE WORST ECONOMIC CLIMATE WAS ONE OF THE CONTRIBUTING FACTORS TO MY BECOMING AN ENTREPRENEUR

Without facing one of the hardest, most depressing times of my life during my most impressionable years, there is a chance I would not be where I am today. You probably recognize this period of time as the Great Recession that hit the globe hard from 2008 to 2009.

Where I grew up, our local economy was heavily impacted by the city next door: Atlantic City, New Jersey. Almost everyone in my hometown worked in Atlantic City or had a job directly tied to the city's success. For those who are unfamiliar with Atlantic City, the best way to describe it is as a hand-me-down version of Las Vegas on the beach.

During a recession, one of the very first things that individuals cut out of their daily expenses are the nonessentials, such as entertainment. Unfortunately, Atlantic City and our entire local economy was based on that one industry alone. Once people could no longer afford their mortgages and necessities in life, visits to Atlantic City were quickly deducted from their expenses. Why gamble away whatever little you have left when you have so much debt and limited disposable income?

Soon after, as one can easily expect, casinos began to cut any "nonessential expenses" they could spare, which meant massive layoffs, and soon, full-on closures. Entertainers, executives, dealers, servers, cleaners, cooks, customer service representatives—any job you could think of—all faced the same harsh reality. It seemed like everyone was out of a job and would be for a long time.

I can still remember hearing from some of my closest childhood friends that their parents' homes had been foreclosed on. I can still see some of the local businesses I grew up with closing up shop, as our town's population began to shrink. I will never forget my father working three different jobs at one point to support our struggling family.

I can't recall another period in my life that was so bleak. The best word to describe the feel of everything was "exhaustion." Everyone walked around like zombies, and everyone had the same doom-and-gloom mindset that it would only get worse. For those who could work, they'd work until they had nothing left in the tank. For those who couldn't work, it was either fight or flight.

AT THE TIME, I WAS YOUR STEREOTYPICAL, AVERAGE SUBURBAN SIXTEEN-YEAR-OLD

For some reason, I thought that having the longest hair possible without needing to brush it was fashionable. My clothing of choice was jeans and a zip-up hoodie that was always one size larger than it should have been. My only real possessions were my laptop (which started as a family laptop and within a few weeks became mine exclusively) and a digital camera that had been given to me as a birthday gift a year earlier.

Except for school and working as a busboy at the local

Red Robin, the majority of my time was spent chatting in online forums (or message boards, as they were known then). I first stumbled upon AOL chat rooms and AOHell (a popular AOL hacking tool) in the mid-nineties. Then came Yahoo! GeoCities in the late nineties, Macromedia (now Adobe) Fireworks, Myspace layouts, and finally, message boards in the early 2000s.

I loved interacting with people online, and it was through these experiences that I learned that my calling was making things for other people. When I was twelve or thirteen years old, I created a fan site for my favorite local theme park, Six Flags Great Adventure in Jackson, New Jersey. This not only became the most popular theme park fan site on the internet at its prime, but it also replaced Six Flags as the number one search result in the early days of Google. By the time I turned sixteen, I knew I wanted to create something that was digital and make some actual money doing it.

Still, I wouldn't characterize this as wanting to be an entrepreneur—not yet. It was a mixture of being a naive teenager wanting to demonstrate my own independence, while also doing something that I deeply enjoyed (unlike working as a busboy at the local Red Robin).

THE VERY FIRST MOMENT THAT LED TO MY ACCIDENTAL ENTREPRENEURSHIP

It was mid-July 2009, in the later part of the morning, and I was spending time in the basement of one of my childhood best friends, Kegan Gilbert. We initially became friends out of proximity—he was the only friend I could walk to without having to beg one of my parents to drive me over to his house, as we both lived on the same street—but later bonded over our love for computers, software, websites, and message boards. As Kegan played *Castle Crashers* on his Xbox, I mindlessly browsed the internet, trying to think, *What should I do? What could I do? What could I be good at?*

Sometimes a random thought just pops into your head. You could be taking a walk, you could be reading a book... anything. And that random thought can spark a firework in your head. This happened to me while I was aimlessly browsing the internet that day. I started thinking, *Do any of the local businesses in our area have websites?* I tried searching online for all of the local businesses I knew around my town and couldn't find anything. Except for a basic landing page every now and then, not a single small business had a website of its own. It's hard to believe now, but it wasn't normal for a small local business to have its own website back then. And then it suddenly clicked. I realized I could make websites for the local businesses I thought needed them (which, to me, was automatically everyone who didn't have one).

When a firework lights off in my brain, I become—at least briefly—uncontrollably obsessed with the idea. It's something that has carried over the years—my team at Chop Dawg can tell you it is both my most wonderful and my most annoying trait.

I looked for domain names to register. Kegan joined me and we debated over names for a solid hour. I wanted the name Chop Shop—I wanted something to sound "badass." He kept pushing Top Dog, as a way to clearly communicate to customers who is the best. We kept going back and forth until we compromised.

"How about Chop Dog?"

"Yeah, that sounds good."

It turned out "Chop Dog" wasn't available to purchase as a domain name, but another similar name was "Chop Dawg."

As a sixteen-year-old, I liked the wordplay. Kegan also liked it because it would only make the company stand out further from the crowd. It helped, too, that where we grew up in New Jersey, many people had a slight accent, and when they pronounced "dog," it came out "dawg" anyway.

One click of the computer mouse later, and www.Chop-

Dawg.com, the very same company that I run today, was born.

At that moment, without even realizing it, I became an accidental entrepreneur.

NOW I NEEDED MY FIRST CUSTOMER

If you haven't visited New Jersey in the summertime, let me paint a picture for you. First, it is hot. Quite hot. You're looking at temperatures between the high eighties and low hundreds. Second, it is humid. Within five to ten minutes of being outside, you're covered in a gallon of sweat. It isn't the most pleasant of experiences, to put it lightly.

Unfortunately for my sixteen-year-old self, I didn't have the luxury of driving around in an air-conditioned car to deliver my pitch to the local businesses. Instead, I walked. And keep in mind, this wasn't the city life, where everything was walking distance. This was the suburban life, where you would walk miles to your nearest shopping center, as it was intended for you to drive to.

Kegan would usually tag along for moral support. I also hoped that with him being slightly older than me, these business owners would take us more seriously. Unfortunately for me, Kegan looked younger than his age. Oh well, at least I had the company on those long, sweltering summer days.

Every morning, we would leave my house around nine o'clock (the time most local businesses opened up) and visit each individual shopping center, going door to door to pitch my website design services to these businesses. I was confident they would see I could be a savior to their business in this harsh economic climate.

Imagine a sweaty sixteen-year-old who has no idea how to appropriately dress, walking door to door and asking to speak to the person in charge. He wants to pitch his services and make his services known. Imagine him somehow getting in front of that person in charge, trying to sell web design for the first time in his life, without any proper presentation. Now imagine another teenager following along who just stood there during the pitch, without saying a word. It was an awkward situation every time. Needless to say, I scored zero sales.

IN HINDSIGHT, THERE WAS A TON WRONG WITH MY "PLAN" OF ATTACK

It wasn't just the awkwardness I put these people through that was the big problem. Today, having a website is almost viewed as a necessity. But back in 2009, many small businesses thought of websites as *accessories*, not necessities.

That mentality, mixed with a terrible economic climate, meant that almost immediately, everyone mentally dismissed the idea of such an "accessory." I had many small local business owners kindly explain to me, "I've been in business for X years without a website, and I've been fine! Why would I need one now?" I honestly couldn't come up with a defense. To me, a website was a no-brainer. I could not grasp how some people did not feel the need for a website.

Over time, though, I began picking up subtle cues from the business owners I spoke to. I started to identify what they wanted to hear and what they didn't. I also started figuring out what type of clothing I should wear to make people want to listen to me—just by changing my attire alone, I had fewer owners pointing at their "Do Not Solicit" signs. I was *determined* to make this work. I knew, deep down, that I was going to find my first customer. I had the mindset that for every no I was hearing, I was getting closer to that first yes. From there, I told myself, the rest would be history.

It's the one feeling I wish I still had today. Today, even when I am feeling confident, there is always a small voice in my head that has a shred of doubt. It's because I know I have so far left to go on this journey. On one hand, I love it, as this little shred of doubt keeps me grounded and always working harder. On the other hand, there was something so amazing about that time before becoming jaded by the daily grind. It's that "naive optimism," as Treehouse founder Ryan Carson called it. I miss that feeling.

AND THEN, SOMEHOW, STRAIGHT OUT OF FOLKLORE, *SOMETHING JUST HAPPENED*

It was August 31, 2009, the final day of my summer vacation before my junior year of high school began, and Kegan and I were down to the final shopping center. These were the last few businesses in the entire town that I had yet to pitch to. First, there were only five remaining, then four, three, two...finally, I had one shop left before I could say that I had officially struck out, spending my entire summer pitching my services that no one wanted.

This last shop was a small pet boutique and grooming service called It's a Doggie Dog World. It was a perfect fit, in my head at least. I remember thinking it was a sign: *They're all about dogs, and our company has the name "Dawg" in it.* This was obviously meant to be. Kegan thought I was crazy when I said this out loud. (He was probably right.)

Kegan and I put on that look of confidence we'd gotten accustomed to wearing over the previous month and a half, walked in, and went to the very first employee we could find. There was only one in the entire store, right at the checkout register. As it turned out, he wasn't an employee but one of the co-owners of the shop, Michael Baker.

The entire store was painted blue, with red accent walls every few feet and plants laid out. It all set the mood for what the customer could expect when walking in. It was one of the nicest, most put-together small shops we had walked into all summer. Michael was behind his register, speaking to a customer; he paused, looked right at us, and asked what we wanted. I explained briefly I wanted to offer him a website, and he immediately said he was with a customer and that he could talk to us once he was done with her.

We were used to being told no or go away, so this was one of the best responses we had ever gotten. A small victory already.

I wasn't going to waste my last at-bat. Once the customer had left the store, which, candidly, felt like hours (although in reality was just minutes), I pitched to Michael exactly what I was capable of, why I was the guy for the job, and how I could help his business. In response, Michael began discussing how disappointed he was with his current website, how he couldn't update it, how it looked terrible and didn't reflect his store. All of a sudden, I didn't need to sell myself to him anymore. Having a website was not an accessory for him; he felt it was a *necessity*, too.

I told him, without any hesitation, I could resolve every-thing he had mentioned.

He looked at me, at Kegan, then back at me again, asking, "How much?"

Whoops! I hadn't thought about how much I'd charge for this as a service. I had been so occupied with finding a paying customer that I hadn't thought of the price I would want anyone to pay. One of the most make-or-break fun-damentals of business was something that I now needed to decide on the fly. I blurted out, "Two hundred dollars."

I really didn't know what to charge or where even to begin. Was $200 too much? Too little? Do small businesses spend $200 on their expenses? Two hundred dollars was a lot of money, right? How much do small businesses spend a month on expenses?

My mind was still racing when Michael said, "It's a deal." He shook my hand and asked how soon I could have some-thing for him. I officially had my first customer.

EARLY IN MY JOURNEY, I RECEIVED ONE OF THE MOST INFORMATIVE, IMPACTFUL TELEPHONE CALLS OF MY LIFE

Known as the first "T-shirt bakery," Johnny Cupcakes has one of the strongest followings for a small brand that I have seen. Its founder, Johnny Earle, started selling T-shirts out of the trunk of his beat-up '89 Toyota Camry and ended up owning a store, designed to resemble a real bakery, that sells cupcake-themed T-shirts to people from all around the country. He designed each store to be an unforgettable experience imitating the old-fashioned bakery environment—displaying T-shirts in vintage industrial refrigerators and on baking racks, using pastry boxes as packaging, and even making the store smell like frosting! Customers always left with not just a great T-shirt but also with a story to tell their friends. Johnny was able to create something out of nothing and build a brand that was so valuable to his customers that they were willing to wait hours in line to buy a shirt; some were willing to get his company's logo tattooed on themselves.

I was fortunate enough to discover this brand back in my very early teenage years. Learning about the story of a young man who had dropped out of college, created a T-shirt as a joke, and ended up starting a multimillion-dollar company left an impact on me. I can't recall how Johnny heard about me or how he even got my phone number, but one day he called me. I was starstruck. He spent a solid thirty minutes speaking to me on the phone, setting the early expectations of what entrepreneurship was all about. Johnny acted as a mentor to me that day and, today, still serves as a linchpin that I give significant credit to in helping me shape my own entrepreneurial career.

One of the things that resonates with me to this day was Johnny's explanation of how he grew his business. He called it the *snowball effect.*

"Imagine," he said, "taking a small snowball on top of a hill and pushing it down. It will start collecting more and more snow as it continues to roll down the hill, picking up pace. If the hill is long enough, eventually it'll be the size of a boulder. Businesses should be built the same way. Impress one customer so that they tell two. Have those two tell two more. You now have a snowball rolling down that hill."

Within a few weeks after that first meeting with Michael at his shop, I had his website completed. It was my crowning achievement to date. I had designed the website to look state of the art and to match the company's already gorgeous branding. I went to the store after school a couple of times, using my digital camera to take high-quality photos of the entire space. I coded the website myself and worked with Michael to ensure the content on the website flowed flawlessly. I was proud, and he was impressed.

About one month later, the website was a smashing success. Not only did they love the look of it, but it was *producing results.* It was making the store money. Michael was ecstatic. He told me that since we'd launched their new website, new customers were flocking to the store and revenue was growing. In a recession, I had helped him to do *better* business. This was it—cue the happiness explosion.

After that, step one to Johnny Earle's snowball effect was complete: *make the customer want to tell everyone about what you do.*

What I didn't know at the time was just how valuable their happiness and eagerness to tell the world was going to be. I was hoping for maybe one or two referrals, but I got much luckier than that. It turned out to be a quickly rolling snowball. Michael and his co-owner, Brian Jackson, began calling every entrepreneur they knew to talk about Chop Dawg and told them to hire me "as soon as possible" before I became overbooked. (I loved the vague urgent deadline they added to that—it really did make it sound like I was in demand, which consequently, thanks to them, I quickly became.)

My phone was now ringing nonstop, and emails were coming in, all because I had done great work for one well-connected client who knew a lot of other like-minded people eager to buy in. Ironically, many of the small businesses that called were the same ones that had said no to me just a few months prior. In fact, the majority of them were—only they were ready to pay attention to me now.

FOR THE FIRST SEVERAL MONTHS, I WAS TAKING ON AN INCREDIBLY EXHILARATING BUT FLAT-OUT *UNSUSTAINABLE* DAILY ROUTINE

I get why a lot of great entrepreneurs struggle in school. For the remaining two years of high school, only my body was truly there. From 6:00 a.m. until 2:30 p.m. every day, I would sit in class while thinking about the work that I wanted to do after school let out.

When I did make it home, I'd grab a quick bite to eat, sit at my makeshift desk in my childhood bedroom, and begin working. I realized early on that most of my clients closed by 5:00 p.m., so I had a small window to reach them. The rest of my time, until late in the evening, was dedicated to Chop Dawg work. By the time I clocked off at 1:30 or 2:30 a.m., it was only due to the fact that I could no longer keep my eyes open, not because my to-do list had dried up. Weekday after weekday, I would get by on a few hours of sleep and typically divide the weekends between being on the grind and catching up on sleep.

I WENT FROM TWO TO FOUR CLIENTS, TO EIGHT CLIENTS, TO SIXTEEN CLIENTS, TO THIRTY-TWO CLIENTS WITHIN ONLY A FEW MONTHS

What had begun as an introduction to small businesses from Michael and Brian turned into every one of my early clients introducing me to their friends, colleagues, and partners. Soon enough, I was getting telephone calls and introductions from businesses in Virginia, Arizona, across the entire eastern coast of the United States, and even internationally, with my first Canadian client. I couldn't keep up with the demand—I had clients paying me in advance to sit on a waiting list as a "good faith" deposit. I was even able to raise my prices, and small businesses were still willing to pay.

Even though I know way better now, I really felt like I was starting a little mini-empire. And somehow, I was able to keep up with the demand for my services—I hadn't hired a single person yet.

Then one day, I received an email from my local newspaper, *The Current of Egg Harbor Township*, asking to interview me. The email briefly mentioned that they had been hearing about my story for a few months now and thought this could be something fun to share with their readers.

AS A NOW-SEVENTEEN-YEAR-OLD, THERE WAS NO WAY I COULD SAY NO

Not only would appearing in a newspaper inflate my ego—already enormous from my first year of success—but I knew it would only help me attract more customers. It was my first time being interviewed, and on top of that, I was interviewed and photographed in my childhood bedroom (or as I called it at the time, my studio). It was a unique experience, to say the least, having five people and a large camera all crammed into my tiny bedroom to interview me.

On September 23, 2010, my face was on the front page of my local newspaper, with the large headline, "Clients are rolling in for 17-year-old web designer."

This is when the fun truly began. Almost immediately after the article was published, another newspaper reached out. This time, it was the largest newspaper in my area, *The Press of Atlantic City*. Unlike my small hometown paper, everyone in the entire county received this one. Just a few months later, I was again on the front page, this time with the headline, "Egg Harbor Township High School student runs own website design business."

The snowball effect was happening all over again. Every local news station, newspaper, and magazine, wanted to run my story and capitalize on the concept of local teen entrepreneurs while it was still a novelty.

Immediately after my article in *The Press of Atlantic City* was published, NBC South Jersey reached out, requesting to do a news segment on me. NBC Philadelphia soon followed, asking to pick up its South Jersey affiliate's story and have me come in for a live interview broadcast. It was my first time being interviewed on live television, and I wanted something special to wear. I ended up making a terribly designed Chop Dawg T-shirt to represent my company. At the time, I was pretty proud of it.

NBC Philadelphia quickly led to a request from the leading newspaper for Philadelphia, the *Philadelphia Inquirer*. *South Jersey Magazine* had me come up for a photo shoot and interview. AOL picked up my story and ran it across the entire United States. *Inc.* magazine's website shared my story from AOL. All of this happened in less than a few months. The snowball had officially turned into an avalanche.

The day after my NBC Philadelphia interview aired, I remember staying home from school, watching my email inbox explode. Within just a few hours, I had several hundred small businesses reaching out to schedule consultations with me. It got to the point where my email flat-out stopped working, as I had run out of hard disk space.

Before, handling fifty or so small businesses had been exhausting but doable. But growing by a factor of a thousand within a few months' time was a completely different monster. This was the type of coverage that changes the way you think about your position in the world. I felt more important and simultaneously more overwhelmed than I had ever felt before.

A lot of entrepreneurs go through this when they end up doing something worthy of a good story. I recently spoke to my good friend John Boitnott about this media effect on early-stage companies, because he has been a tech writer and journalist for more than twenty years with publications such as *Fast Company, Inc., USA Today,* and *Forbes.* Through his writings, he's seen a wide spectrum of stories and outcomes go by. Suffice it to say, he's seen a lot.

One thing that John has noticed:

> *"There are some startups that, through a combination of networking, hustle, an interesting idea, and a story that works, can get good coverage. What's happening is that the entrepreneur has made contact with journalists and conveyed the idea well. But what happens after the coverage is really up to the startup."*

SO I HAD TWO CHOICES I COULD MAKE

1. I could continue running this business myself, while picking and choosing whom I wanted to work with. Doing this would mean really sacrificing on volume. Unless I could charge a lot per project, I would be missing out on upgrading into a bigger, stronger business.
2. I could try to help as many clients as possible and build a team to support this influx of work. We could take

advantage of all the volume and be able to get our services out much faster.

I chose the latter, and I'm really glad I did.

When you have a small and inconsistent volume coming in, it's almost always better to start out by yourself. But now, the universe had given me a glaring sign, with all the subtlety of a brick being thrown through a window, that it was time to start a real business. This was a sales volume that I had never experienced before, and I couldn't handle it alone—this was my golden opportunity to get a team in order.

According to John, that makes all the difference:

> *"If what you're offering isn't great, then that's the difference. A lot of times, the stereotypical Y Combinator, Techstars, 500 Startups graduate has a good idea and a good beginning. If the people are likable and the idea has a foundation, it can be worked on in the incubator, but many companies are still too early for the media coverage."*

News coverage can be toxic if you don't have a product or service that really fulfills the story that was told about you. Had I not been able to provide the service that the story promised, all the press coverage would have been equivalent to a snake bite, rather than a shot of adrenaline.

I HAD NO IDEA HOW TO FIND AND PUT TOGETHER THE RIGHT TEAM

How exactly does one "hire"? What do you ask? How much do you pay? I remember spending hours reviewing résumés and portfolios and reading online about the proper ways to bring on new people to a growing startup.

The only tools I had in building a team were leveraging my local university's alumni network (I pretended to be a fellow alumnus, when in reality, I was still in high school), asking friends of friends, and reaching into the connections that I had built from my years of running the Six Flags Great Adventure fan site.

Some of those early hires turned out to be not only talented but long lasting. One of my team members, Brandon Teller, became a chief technology officer for me and served at Chop Dawg for almost a decade. Eddie Contento, whom I hired as a chief design officer, worked directly alongside me for years and personally created the Chop Dawg branding still used today. There were also hires who turned out to be hiccups. One of my first hires, a woman named Lindsey, vanished without a trace within a few weeks of working on a project. I also hired a few individuals who turned out to be more dependent, requiring me to hold their hands for the job to be completed.

I also had to figure out how to balance being a full-time college student, closing new work, and managing a team while trying to maintain my overall sanity. As you might expect, it was impossible to manage it all.

But how long would it take for me to admit that?

I DECIDED AFTER ONE AND A HALF SEMESTERS THAT I NEEDED TO QUIT COLLEGE FOR THE GOOD OF THE BUSINESS

At the time, going to college felt like the only decision—everyone else my age was doing it. I enrolled in school to learn business management and marketing. Then one day, I realized I was already doing just that. Moreover, none of my clients were asking for my college degree.

At the same time, a unique opportunity landed in our laps. A local client by the name of PartyHopp reached out to us with a new challenge. They wanted us to build them a *website application,* a project that would need much more functionality than the static websites we had been working on thus far.

That Ryan Carson concept of "naive optimism" hadn't failed me yet. So I said, "Let's do it."

I informed the team that app
There was justifiably some th
team members. Some had b
tine and the steady income l
website work. If the tried-a
us money, why try to change

at we didn't know we had to do,
gnificantly more "high-ticket"
ontracts became a thing. We
our small business services
ald have), but our new target
anding them. We looked like
ontract for a project that had
line.

In hindsight, I should have t
sideration more, but I was u
felt I could do no wrong. Once
I was committed to, that we
others on the team who wer
away, I decided to pull the tr
make the pivot.

was, if you are going to sell a
perations and appearance had
are spending much more of
services, their standards and
considerably.

we finally found someone on
erested but also pressing us
mediately in love. This was

ng for: $200,000 for a *single*
ggering to me. Just two years

For the first time in our co
began to reach a standsti
dip. We had expected it—a
plete 180, and we didn't ha
had with the small busine
bilities. Proving that we c
whole new territory. It wa
for Chop Dawg.

our *entire* gross revenue for
client takes a lot of prepara-
tly what we were in for. We
forth with this new poten-
orable terms to make them
contract, one that, at the end

of the day, should have guaranteed the client would pay us. Everything was lined up and ready to go.

But one thing I've learned through experience is that until the dotted line is signed and the deposit has been received, nothing is a done deal.

RIGHT AT THE TIME WE AGREED TO SIGN THE CONTRACT, THE WOULD-BE CLIENT VANISHED WITHOUT A TRACE

Just like that, all of our months of work and preparation went down the drain with absolutely nothing to show for it. Our team had shrunk drastically, as we didn't have the same volume of work as we used to. If it wasn't for the savings I had kept in place for the company, we would have dissolved totally right then and there.

I felt like a failure, and team morale was perilously low. The positive thoughts that had once played on a loop in my head turned into persistently negative ones. For the first time, I was becoming jealous of the success I saw in others. I kept thinking, we just *had* to do something different. But even through the negative feedback loop, sometimes an idea just pops into your head that makes you think that everything can be fixed.

Why wait for others to build their apps when we could make our own?

Desperate for a paddle, I ran with this idea. This would be the fix. After all, we were constantly waiting for leads to come, to hear back on proposals, on contract edits...why wait any longer? We could show them all and make our own app.

And with that, Subtle was born.

Subtle, as I claimed, would become the one-stop spot for you to control everything you needed online as a small business owner. You could manage your website, your calendar, your emails, your files, your address book, your customer relationships, and your employees all from one central hub. It would be called Subtle because you wouldn't think twice about the technology that would quietly run your business.

I looked at our company bank account: it had about $50,000. I decided this was what I would invest back into my team—it would be as though I was our client. I gave us an August 1, 2013, deadline, eight months from the start of the year and also, coincidentally, the four-year anniversary of Chop Dawg.

But Subtle never ended up launching. We never made a single dollar. I'll go into the many reasons why I failed in chapter 4.

ONE PROBLEM THAT PERSISTED THROUGHOUT MY FIRST FEW YEARS WAS MY UNCONTROLLABLE EGO

After my failure with Subtle, it took me a while to deal with the personal devastation of losing $50,000 and not knowing where to go next. I can't remember a time when I felt more self-loathing than when we pulled the plug on Subtle. I had a hard time dealing with the persistent feelings of self-doubt that plagued me. Previously, even when I had experienced setbacks, I had always believed in myself. Going door to door, being rejected by most store owners, I had always kept going because of my belief that eventually, I was going to arrive at a victory. But I no longer felt like that. I felt like there was no possible way to move forward. I truly believed that I was a failure.

To overcome that defeat, I had to do something that I had never done before: I learned about psychology. Perhaps I could figure out not just what was causing me to feel like I was in an inescapable mind ditch, but I could figure out the mental pains that hold so many others back in entrepreneurship as well.

My endeavor to learn more about psychology introduced me to the study of ego. We tend to use the word "ego" loosely to describe people who are selfish or in it for themselves alone. I learned that I had created my own ego to act unconsciously as a barrier to insulate myself from the rest of the world. It is an unconscious defense mechanism

many ambitious, driven individuals are probably prone to. It's certainly easier to propel yourself forward in the face of major setbacks when nothing is ever your own fault. But in doing so, I was living in "duality" by separating myself and my business success from the reality of others and the world around me.

Living in duality creates a lot of pain for ourselves and those around us. For me, it meant filtering my entire life through a lens of judgment. Things were "right or wrong," "good or bad," "pretty or ugly." But these binary judgments only served to close me off to others. Through all of the decisions that I had made leading up to Subtle's collapse, it had never really mattered what my team wanted.

I see a lot of people who go through this immutable pain today. When things aren't going their way, their lives become centered on judging others, condemning alternatives, and fearing the unknown. Anything within that is perceived as "bad" or "wrong" is suppressed, repressed, and denied. This will lead to burnouts, breakdowns, and alienation.

Struggling entrepreneurs are especially prone to becoming entrenched in this duality, going through anger, depression, paranoia, and anxiety all alone, sometimes succumbing to what is known as "founder depression."

I recently had an insightful chat with my good friend

Michael Gasiorek, who is the codirector of the San Francisco chapter of Startup Grind (which, as he puts it, builds communities that offer the "minimum viable dose of Silicon Valley thinking anywhere in the world"), on how founder depression needs to become more of a discussion in our society than we are presently comfortable with.

Michael told me:

> *"Founder depression should be talked about a lot more. The startup world needs to be encouraging with being open about your emotions—the work culture focused on endless results and not taking care of oneself is unsustainable."*

Research suggests that entrepreneurs are 30 percent more likely to develop depression than their counterparts.

But why is that?

The obvious answer is that they're simply succumbing to the mounting pressures and challenges the globalized economy presents to any new startup in this day and age. But startup stress isn't the only reason so many founders deal with depression. In fact, many simply do not have the personality characteristics necessary to deal with the high stress, loneliness, rejection, and other situations that would make any normal person question what they are doing.

If you are an entrepreneur reading this and dealing with depression, that doesn't necessarily mean you're not cut out for this game. I have dealt with my fair share of anxiety, stress, and even depression at some of my lowest points. I still battle with this today. A successful entrepreneur can experience all this adversity and still continue to fight for their crazy ideas. But that fire to keep pushing forward has to come from within. How you move forward from your most spectacular failures is what separates a failed startup from a successful one, and a failed entrepreneur, at that.

Have you accepted your part in your business's failures? Are you able to accept failure at all? Are you mentally prepared to accept the daily obstacles and setbacks inherent to entrepreneurship?

If not, you'll probably be treading water forever, and maybe this game isn't meant for you. Because, while continued innovations with technology have made creating a new startup venture easier than ever before, it's also never been easier to fail. And *how* to fail is something that should be taught to us at a much younger age.

Michael believes that we should give high school students the opportunity to experience "safe failures" so that it becomes easier to deal with real failure later on. He himself went through depression when things weren't going well with his first business. He would sleep all of the time so he wouldn't have to think about his business or how lonely he felt in it.

Entrepreneurship is inherently lonely and depressing because you are indeed alone on a ledge with your "crazy ideas." So how do we normalize this conversation?

Resources such as Startup Grind offer support groups, and I think this should become a common resource offered to entrepreneurs around the world. Founder depression should simply be talked about more. The startup world needs to be encouraging about being open with one's emotions and taking individual self-care seriously, too—the work culture focused on endless growth in sacrifice of oneself is simply unsustainable in the long run.

WHEN GOING THROUGH FOUNDER DEPRESSION, IT'S HELPFUL TO REMEMBER THAT EGO IS NOT THE ENEMY EITHER

I've read so many books and think-pieces that say the ego is something that needs to be "destroyed." But it was really my use of ego as a way to separate myself from reality that needed to be destroyed.

The framework would not have been possible at all without ego. I could not have created Chop Dawg and kept it in business for the past ten years without ego. All of the

great businesses and products that you use today wouldn't exist without some form of ego in their founding origins. But the difference is that before, I personally used my ego as a shield to protect myself from rejection. Now I use it as a tool.

Ego is not negative or positive. Your thought patterns, positive or negative, will shape the world that your mind creates. A person who is rooted in a positive outlook has a "positive ego," and a person who is rooted in negativity has a "negative ego."

Moving toward having a positive ego puts you in better alignment with reality and, ultimately, in a better position to succeed in entrepreneurship.

I REALIZED THERE ARE COMMON THREADS THAT THE BEST OF THE BEST ENTREPRENEURS SHARE

Duality prevented me from learning valuable lessons from other entrepreneurs because it made me assume what didn't work for others would still work for me because I was somehow "better." I wasn't able to truly learn from my failures because I had never fully accepted responsibility for them. But once I started to force myself to chip away at my sense of duality, I was much more open to learning from others. I no longer felt uncomfortable knowing that I was wrong. Now I simply wanted to know what those who

were actually succeeding were doing to make it. I was in no place to judge anyone. I only wanted to observe, learn, and act on this newfound knowledge.

Just like during my early days going door to door selling websites to small businesses and learning as I went, I needed to pick up on the cues that other entrepreneurs were exhibiting. When you speak to enough successful entrepreneurs in the game, read their books, and listen to their interviews, you can start seeing the common threads—the framework of principles—that make them successful. How you apply those principles is then up to you.

IN THAT SAME CONVERSATION, MICHAEL AND I ASKED OURSELVES, "ARE THERE TOO MANY ENTREPRENEURS?"

Michael was eager to jump into this topic, as it's something he often thinks about. After all, the more entrepreneurs entering the pool, the harder it is to stand out, right?

> *"Yes, let's talk about that bubble. Should you be an entrepreneur? Yes, but only if there is a problem that needs to get solved, you are willing to take the quality of life cut, and if you truly know that starting a company is the BEST way to create a solution. If you can do all of those three things, then be an entrepreneur."*

And that is true! Because the other problem with entrepreneurship is that there are too many people entering the game for the wrong reasons. The desire to become an entrepreneur cannot be based solely on the pursuit of individual success or wealth, because that's a foundation that is more likely to crumble under your own self-hype.

> *"The purpose of entrepreneurship has gotten away from solving actual problems to simply becoming the 'person behind THAT thing.' A lot of college students will graduate and form their own companies. Well-meaning friends of the first-time entrepreneurs are encouraging them to start companies rather than joining existing teams."*

This ends up creating a bit of a paradox. When everyone wants to be a leader, who will then work collectively to make sure ideas become reality? If everyone wants to be the "starter of things," then who will be doing the joining? We'll explore these questions in the next chapter, where we'll dive deeper into the implications of the New Economy.

CHAPTER 2

WHAT IS THE NEW ECONOMY?

In 2005, it was out of necessity rather than opportunity that Phillip Walker founded his company, Network Solutions Provider. (What a getting-down-to-business name!)

Phillip had been the vice president of an IT company but left after disagreeing with other executives about the direction of the business. He'd had it up to here with others not seeing what he saw: the challenges that companies across the country had with installing and managing their phone and internet systems. He looked for other jobs, but his mentor suggested that he start a business of his own. He had talked to plenty of clients who'd told him their needs, so why not just go out on his own? Confident that he could provide a direct one-to-one solution and get rid of the middleman, he dived in. But despite his contacts, he couldn't find any real sales leads.

Phillip tried finding customers by going door to door. He visited office parks unannounced and asked IT managers about their phone and internet services. He convinced them of their need and persuaded even the most apprehensive to become customers. When reading about Phillip's experiences, I immediately felt a connection to my own. Most people would give up, but not Phillip. This was Phillip's opportunity to craft his message. However, he faced another obstacle to success. Much of his company's credibility and ability to scale would depend on securing "the big partnerships" with the enormous telecom companies.

I also faced this issue when I was trying to go for bigger clients. Big clients, just like I had found, are willing to spend big money on those they feel they can trust. It's hard to convince the big business clients to trust you without an existing portfolio of big business clients. Chasing the big business client wasn't going to work. So Phillip came up with a plan: he focused his attention on the midsize companies instead.

We often celebrate the big companies, the whales of companies. Others in Phillip's industry were all trying to go for the whales, so he found many midsize businesses that were very much willing to test his services. He was able to grow his customer base while courting telecoms at the same time. He spent eight months trying to win over Tele-Pacific, a big telecom company in California and Nevada. He visited the office three times and gave presentations. Each presentation became clearer, and the proof was mounting because he was acquiring clients at the same time. After the third presentation, he nabbed TelePacific's business. By 2007, he landed a partnership with AT&T. By 2012, Network Solutions Provider had $6.1 million in sales and twenty-four full-time employees.

This story of Phillip Walker is a formula of sorts for entrepreneurs all around the globe.

1. He found a need for companies across the country. This was 2005, so this was still the beginning of the push by many corporations to start modernizing their infrastructure. Phillip sensed a need. How and with whom were they going to install and manage these new phone and internet systems?
2. He had a solution, and his employer didn't agree with the need for these services, so he left and started his own company.
3. He needed to find the right companies to speak to. Big businesses weren't cutting it because he couldn't build enough trust yet to make a sale. So he went to medium-sized companies that knew of the need and were more willing to trust.
4. He needed to convince those right people that he was

the one. In order to do that, he needed tangible proof that he was the one for the job. So he gave presentations and kept fine-tuning his message until it really spoke to people.

5. The timing was right. As I said, this was 2005. He saw the need before others came to the same conclusion.

Entrepreneurs today have a vast set of tools at their disposal to reach people. Phillip Walker, on the other hand, didn't have YouTube, Facebook, Twitter, or LinkedIn as advertising channels yet. There were still plenty of creative ways to advertise, but nothing as easy as having instant access to thousands of people who can share your message. But this didn't matter anyway, as Phillip didn't even have the budget to put an ad in the Yellow Pages.

But Phillip has two qualities that have defined entrepreneurs for generations, with and without technology: the insatiable desire to understand the pain points and offer real solutions.

According to John Boitnott (my journalist friend mentioned in chapter 1), there are essentially two types of people in the world:

1. People who have woken up to the idea that there is a larger world out there and that they can contribute value to it in some way

While it's impossible to summarize the New Economy in just one sentence, an economy truly is made of *people* and the decisions that they make, and those decisions influence the ways they trade with each other.

BREAKING DOWN THE NUTS AND BOLTS OF THE ECONOMY

For many people, the economy may feel like an unfair, rigged system that they have no part of. According to a study released in May 2018 by the United Way ALICE Project, nearly 51 million households don't earn enough to afford the necessities, such as food and housing. That's 43 percent of American households who, if you say the economy is booming right now, are going to want to smack you in the face.

But on the other side of the coin, anyone can strike it rich if they can make all of the right moves. *Really* rich. The myth is that the riches are reserved for big corporations, industrial barons, and lucky startups. In reality, there are many entrepreneurs who have made fortunes but who don't make the news. Too often, people resign when they feel like forces are acting against them. But I think the real barrier that those people need to overcome is that perceived lack of financial freedom. So many people think about money, but few feel that they have the power to make any real decisions for themselves with it. Some feel like there is no hope they can ever acquire the money they need to do anything serious. And while there are economic forces that are working against you, it's also cheaper than ever to start a business (especially online).

HOW I'VE COME TO UNDERSTAND THE THREE FORCES THAT DIRECT THE ECONOMY

In my opinion, a healthy economy is one in which many people feel like they have a hand in the system and are producing something of value and making money doing it.

Here are the three main forces of the economy with a big effect on entrepreneurship:

- **Supply and demand**. Do people actually want what you're selling? How much are they willing to pay for it? People are the deciders of your pricing. The bigger the group of people, the more you can adjust.
- **The business cycle**. Are people at large in the mood to invest, or do they need to save? Do people have money to spend? What are they collectively spending money on? Different industries and niches have their own business cycles. So for your specific industry, a business cycle may be really small. Whether there's excitement in investing in something new (such as cryptocurrencies) or the collective desire for a sought-after product (such as Beanie Babies—remember them?), the cycles themselves are big and small, pow-

ered by human desire. Some are short; others last a long time. With some business cycles, it's hard to tell you're even in them until they're done.

- **Inflation, deflation, and interest rates**. Because running a business requires money, the value of your dollar really matters. How much has the cost of goods gone up? How is access to the credit market? Looking out for these types of swings can be a barometer you can use to keep an eye on external factors affecting your business's financial health.

SUPPLY AND DEMAND

I tend to hear emotionally distant explanations for what supply and demand are. What do I mean by emotionally distant? I hear figures about users, the sales numbers, the shortages, and the demand pricing, but what I don't hear about is the people themselves who collectively decide what is hot and what is not. It's human desire that really powers demand, after all. How many people want your product or service, and how much do they want it? How much would they be willing to pay for it? It comes down to understanding exactly *what* the demand really is, how your supply can fit the demand, and who is demanding your supply.

Over the years, I've constantly tinkered with defining my supply to meet the demand. With Chop Dawg, my supply is my team's expertise and labor availability, and the demand comes directly from the clients. There are outside and inside factors that have determined how I price my supply to fit the demand, but in the end, I've discovered the best approach is through balancing what is good for our company and what is good for the clients. I will never gouge anyone, but I also make sure that our profit margins are secure while covering all labor costs.

I've personally followed the belief that in pricing, if a customer asks you to lower your costs, and you say yes, it means that either you were extorting them or are now undercutting yourself or your team. Both options are unacceptable. When it comes to pricing, there is a sweet spot that is fair, reasonable, and transparent for all parties involved.

Because my supply is my team's expertise, I need to gauge just how *much* my team can fit a client's demand. Is that client looking for a skillset that is easy or hard to find? That influences price, but I always try to keep prices within range or below my competitors, too. It's key to price things fairly, while still being aware of the value you have to give. And because the supply itself is my team, I'm always trying to up the quality by hiring new talent with hard-to-find expertise. If you are selling a physical product, you need to find that supply equilibrium that works for you and also keeps your customers happy.

How much demand you can fulfill with your supply will always be an ongoing question. But sometimes, having too much demand and too little supply will also blow up in your face.

SARAH RIBNER AND JESS EDELSTEIN, THE FOUNDERS OF THE NATURAL DEODORANT COMPANY PIPERWAI KNOW THIS STORY VERY WELL

I had the opportunity to meet with both women in person, because their office is right here in my home city of Philadelphia. PiperWai is a natural deodorant made without harmful ingredients such as parabens, aluminum, and synthetic fragrances—basically, without any of the harmful chemicals in most deodorants on the market today. It's made out of charcoal, and the women's passion for making a product they'd want to use themselves certainly shows when you get your hands on it. Packaged in a teal wrapped glass jar, the soft gray charcoal looks—and smells—more like a fancy candle than a morning hygiene standby.

While Sarah and Jess sensed an opportunity to be trailblazers in the natural deodorant industry, it's grown to be a big business now. Timing! When founding the company, PiperWai started out less as a "business plan" and more as a well-thought-out product. They didn't take the top-down approach of starting a company like some do. It was the ground-up approach—the innovative product came first.

Sales started out slowly. Sometimes they'd get only one sale per day, but once they got their first vendor who was willing to sell PiperWai, they were on the right track and seeing solid sales.

And while Sarah and Jess knew what they wanted their product to be, they could not predict the road map that their company was going to follow. They did not predict, for example, that they'd get on *Shark Tank*. They'd applied to be on that show pretty casually.

And then *Shark Tank* happened. They'd assumed that with the post-show bump, they would need to prepare 10,000 orders. But as people were watching the show and became enamored with the product, Sarah and Jess quickly found that they really underestimated the impact of the post-*Shark Tank* bump—instead of 10,000 orders, they ended up getting 100,000. It was a number that was astronomically off from their expectations. This was not a cause for celebration. There was no way they could keep up with the demand, and that put them in a really stressful spot.

Unable to keep up with the demand, they needed to go through two different copackers, one of which ended up churning out a lower-quality product, which was unacceptable. The copackers had taken shortcuts, and the texture of the deodorant irritated people's skin. For some, it just didn't feel like the PiperWai that they had been expecting. And they were right; it wasn't. But Sarah and Jess constantly chipped away at making sure that everyone's problems were solved, no matter how much time it took every day. Through some excruciating growing pains, Sarah and Jess ended up learning a lot, not only about new ways that they could copack but also that they needed to lay down the law when it came to their vendors.

They ended up finding a much better production partner and were able to satisfy all of that unforeseen demand within six months of the *Shark Tank* bump. They learned that the key to keeping customers happy during turbulent times was to focus on the relationship. Both Jess and Sarah would personally email every customer, offering their empathy, resourcefulness, and warmth. Even some of their angrier customers would switch to being thrilled once they knew they were talking to the actual founders of the company. It was this personal touch that really helped them hang on to many customers who otherwise would have fled. After the six months of hell were over, the company was stronger than ever, with a very loyal new following.

Demand can be lost, but demand can also be recovered. This experience taught the founders of PiperWai how to operate their company at the highest level of stress. As a result, they now have an intimate understanding of how much their company can produce and how not to exceed their own production limits.

THE ECONOMY IS DYNAMIC. IT EXPANDS AND IT CONTRACTS. THIS IS WHAT'S CALLED A BUSINESS CYCLE

Expansion and contraction of the economy is measured by the gross domestic product (GDP). According to the World Bank, in 2016 the United States' GDP was $18.62 trillion. Now, that doesn't equate to how much the goods and services produced were truly worth. It's impossible to really measure the economy with one number—GDP doesn't tell you all that much unless you take a deeper look into what is making the money.

When the GDP continues to contract year over year, that is when economists start talking about an economic depression. But it is the time when the contraction first begins that we call a recession. At that point, unemployment rises, especially when the big companies that have the biggest stake in the GDP start to fail.

With these failures also come great opportunities, believe it or not. When the economy caves in, there are always pioneers who are able to take advantage of the momentary dip. I was able to do this during the Great Recession with my website business, and it afforded me my low startup costs and limited competition, increasing my odds at the time for success.

Just look at the rush of entrepreneurs in those first few years after the dot-com crash. Back then, there were few first-time investors to contribute to the new wave of internet-based companies, limiting the potential for investment to a smaller pool of individuals. That has changed over time. In today's crowded playing field, even the most talented and well-connected entrepreneur is more likely to churn out in the cycle and fail within their first year.

This churn-out actually does provide a benefit, according to Michael Gasiorek:

> *"With too many founders, too many egos, and too many people wanting to start things rather than join things, there needs to be more of a balance to the system. Entrepreneurs that join promising companies after they fail and apply their learned lessons are a great way to balance out the system."*

I see here a parallel to the same issues that happen with oversupply and under-demand. The system needs to be balanced, and not everyone can (or even should) lead. With too much individualism, nothing good gets done; and with too much collectivism, there's no innovation. There has to be a balance.

IT'S EASY TO SEE THESE ECONOMIC CYCLES IN PERSPECTIVE WHEN THEY'RE "ZOOMED OUT" OVER TIME

It's much harder when you're watching them in the short

term. It's like interpreting signs in a crop circle; it's next to impossible to observe any shapes from the ground. But viewed from high above, the pattern is clear.

The economy itself is built entirely on faith. After all, stock market crashes and bank collapses are the result of panic from mass selling and cash withdrawals. Inflation can occur through monetary policies by the Federal Reserve, such as printing more money so that the value of each dollar is worth less. It can also occur through increased demand, such as when a product that once cost you very little is priced very high now that it's highly sought after. (Think of every Christmas season's hottest toy—suddenly you're paying a stranger on Amazon $100 for it, shipping not included.) Inflation has a direct effect on your buying power as a consumer and a would-be entrepreneur. Sometimes inflation can actually be healthy, because it drives up the demand for your product. Healthy inflation also encourages people to spend money instead of sitting on it.

Inflation and deflation are tough because over time, people just expect higher and lower prices for things. When your grandparents tell you how much less things used to cost, they're not lying. But then again, there are things that have gotten cheaper, dollar for dollar, to offset some of that. Just look at how much cheaper computers are today. Yes, some things actually become cheaper *despite* inflation, because their individual cost to produce can go down.

But many of us who are alive now have never experienced a big swing of inflation. Ask your parents, and you'll likely get stories from the 1970s. You'll see in the graph that the value of the dollar is measured by gold. In the early seventies, we were taken off the gold standard (our dollar was backed by gold, and now it's backed by faith), so that accounts for the major drop.

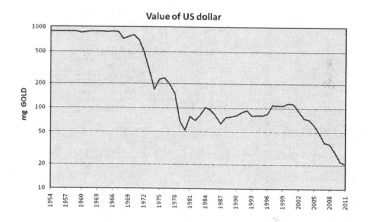

Value of US dollar

Today, a dollar is a printed note that you should consider a standardized IOU that everyone accepts. But how everyone accepts your dollar will change, and you'll feel those changes even if you feel disconnected from big economic shifts. Now let's measure this relative to one dollar. This is the purchasing power of your dollar over time:

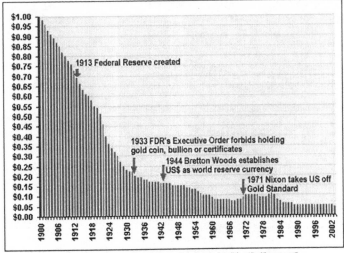

Purchasing Power of the US Dollar (1900 - 2003)

1913 Federal Reserve created

1933 FDR's Executive Order forbids holding gold coin, bullion or certificates

1944 Bretton Woods establishes US$ as world reserve currency

1971 Nixon takes US off Gold Standard

© 2003 Mary Puplava, Financial Sense. Data Source: http://sh.net/hmit/ppowerusd/

The other thing to look out for is interest rates, because this will affect your ability to get credit or a loan for your business and your interest or mortgage rates. If any of your loans are fixed, that means that despite a big economic shift, you won't be paying a higher interest rate in the future. They'll stay the same. And if your loans are variable, you'll feel the swing unless you can refinance or pay off your debt, because your interest rates will keep going up.

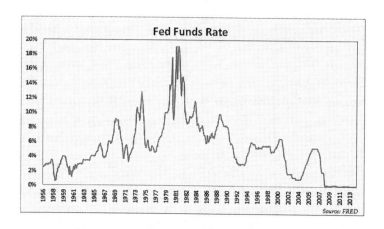

Fed Funds Rate

Source: FRED

You'll see that the numbers tend to line up with economic crises. This graph goes to 2013, when interest rates bottomed out. This was one of the greatest times for getting credit. Low interest rates also greatly increased the supply of money. This is the reason it's so easy to get credit if you have credit history, because the Federal Reserve can lend more money to banks to readily give out loans. Slowly (but surely), the interest rate is now being driven up by the Federal Reserve. When interest rates are increased, the money supply is tightened and the opposite occurs. Only time will tell how high rates will go again, but you can see that they are a force to be reckoned with. Some say that the chair of the Federal Reserve could be considered the most powerful person on the planet.

CREATING VALUE FIRST, WEALTH SECOND

For many years, I really didn't care much about creating

true value for my clients, which now as I type this, makes me cringe. For me, business was only about creating wealth. I wanted satisfied customers for sure, but I didn't care much for the value of what we were creating for them. I was pretty good at generating a pretty small amount of wealth (I did save up $50,000 for Subtle by the time I was twenty), but I didn't have much value to show for myself up to that point.

This wealth-only mindset leads to a narrow view of success. If success is money, then what else is there? I see the chase that some entrepreneurs have for the big acquisition to end it all, and is that all there is? No, of course not. It's great to make money, but the wealth-only mindset misses the key opportunity to truly help others.

Finding something valuable to give to the New Economy is not necessarily about creating something that's *new* either. It can really be about helping the person who had been previously ignored, the customer whom no one else was looking for. Being adventurous with the markets and looking for people who have been ignored in some way is a win-win. My friend Lisa Wang and I recently talked about this very topic.

Lisa is a four-time US National Champion rhythmic gymnast who started SheWorx to close the funding gap that women entrepreneurs face. By empowering more than

20,000 women entrepreneurs around the world, she is surely chipping away at that gap. Through SheWorx, many women have been matched with investor funding. As Lisa pointed out to me, the common misconception many entry-level entrepreneurs have is the necessity to go for the biggest market possible. Instead, she advises:

> *"Really ask yourself, what already exists but is being ignored?"*

A great example of this is Pendeza, a company that makes hosiery specifically for women with darker skin tones. Believe it or not, dark-skinned women were not really thought about in the hosiery market until pretty recently. Pendeza was one of the first brands of hosiery in the United Kingdom made specifically for women with darker skin, and it was only formed in 2011. Instead of coming up with something completely new, the founders identified a group of people who were underrepresented in an industry and created a new opportunity to serve them.

In a similar vein, by first curating samples of their products for people to try, Birchbox found that their customers actually bought *more*. The company built its success by discovering and serving an entirely new market segment: the discerning multitasker. Cofounder Katia Beauchamp discovered, through an extensive market segmentation study, that customers felt like they had *too many* choices when it came to beauty products. There is an overwhelming variety of beauty products on the market, and that volume (as well as the cost of products) turns off many potential customers. So Birchbox filled in the gap. What Birchbox was offering was essentially access to the same beauty products, but their approach of how they sold those products was totally flipped by offering a subscription-based curation of beauty products for clients to try based on their wants and likes, gathered through feedback from previous products received in the "box."

WHEN PEOPLE BEMOAN THE HIGH COST OF GETTING A NEW COMPUTER OR PHONE, I ALWAYS ASK THEM, "DO YOU HAVE ANY IDEA HOW MUCH THESE THINGS USED TO COST?"

While our cost of living has generally risen, technological components are astonishingly more affordable today than they used to be.

As an example, let's look at the cost of a computer's internal storage. Yes, costs have fluctuated and it hasn't felt completely linear, but over time they have gotten a lot cheaper. It is *astonishing*. This has been one of the many reasons that computers are so much more inexpensive today. It's why you don't have to pay $1 million to have a computer that you probably would have had to pay $1 million for back in the eighties.

The graph below, created by John C. McCallum, a former computer science professor from the National University of Singapore, maps out just how much this cost has declined. The technical terms and the numbers here don't matter as much as just soaking in that *massive* downward trend on the graph. It's this and many other things that impact the cost of being connected today.

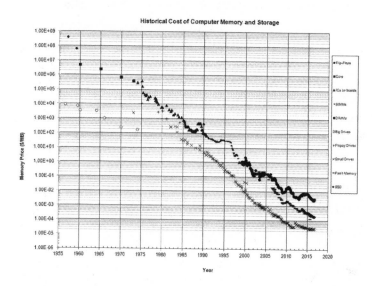

I always think about the things that have allowed us to advance so quickly with our computing power, and afford-able RAM has had one of the biggest impacts. And there are so many more reasons that we are in the spot we are in right now—the true beginning of the New Economy.

LET'S THINK ABOUT WHAT WE WERE DREAMING UP IN THE LATE 1940S INTO THE 1950S

We've been "thinking about the future" for what feels like a long time. I think it became really popularized in the 1950s when the United States was making leaps and bounds in the technological innovations department: flying cars, efficient appliances, robots, a *Jetsons*-style society...Wow, we were really dreaming. The doo-wop branding aesthetic (yes, the same aesthetic found on the cover of this book... wink, wink) defined this era and the big dreams and ideas that came with it. But if you look at the images of this dream, you'll start to notice things that are clearly *missing* from that era's vision of the future. There was so much we couldn't predict based on the frame of reference we had at the time.

Take a hard look at this image below, which was featured in the *Chicago Tribune* back in 1958.

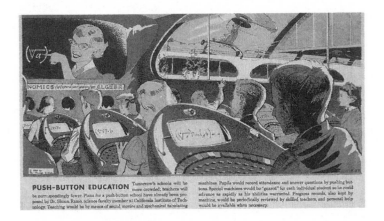

PUSH-BUTTON EDUCATION Tomorrow's schools will be more crowded; teachers will be correspondingly fewer. Plans for a push-button school have already been proposed by Dr. Simon Ramo, science faculty member at California Institute of Technology. Teaching would be by means of sound movies and mechanical tabulating machines. Pupils would record attendance and answer questions by pushing buttons. Special machines would be "geared" for each individual student so he could advance as rapidly as his abilities warranted. Progress records, also kept by machine, would be periodically reviewed by skilled teachers, and personal help would be available when necessary.

The theoretical concept of individualized, adaptive learning dreamed up here has already occurred—it is administered every day to users of smartphones and computers. But think about what is missing from this image.

One thing that is missing is the smartphone itself. But there's also something even bigger that's missing here. These computers don't have a graphic user interface (GUI).

The GUI didn't exist yet, and I doubt many people could visualize the concept at that point. Today, we would use tablets, not these learning "pods." As for smartphones... um, what?

DIGITAL TECHNOLOGY EARLY ON IN THE 1960S AND 1970S BECAME MORE FOCUSED ON THE TOP-DOWN ANALYSIS OF *YOU*

Unless you were working in a lab, digital probably wasn't on your radar in the 1950s. Even if people knew about the concept, until they could see that it was effective in their lives, what was the benefit?

But that all began to change when the government became digital technology's best customer. Computers could be programmed to conduct statistical analyses—demographic data, censuses, elections, you name it—which made them very relevant to the average person's life, especially in the political climate of the 1960s.

Still, these computers were not consumer goods yet. As you saw in one of the previous graphs, the costs associated with computers were through the roof. Only the government and wealthy individuals could afford computers.

Even at this time, tech companies were starting to form, and the internet was also in its infancy. But the cost of the digital technology would need to be much lower in order to market it to consumers. With that financial push from the government, digital technology would eventually have its day.

INTRODUCING DIGITAL TECHNOLOGY TO CONSUMERS WOULD HAPPEN IN WAVES

Computers were originally very confusing to use, and screens did not resemble those of today. One of the big impediments to consumer acceptance of computers was the high learning curve.

Going from line-based commands to the GUI created a fundamental shift in making computers more friendly to consumers.

We went from this (the command line interface)...

```
Command Prompt                                                    _ □ ×

(14) [ ] Online Broadcom NetXtreme and NetXtreme II Firmware Update Utility
         Severity          : Non-Critical
         Reboot            : Not Required
         Update ID         : brcm_fw_nic_2.0.3_windows_32-64

         Update            : b8c1 (#1)
         New Version       : 3.4.4
         Installed Version : 3.4.4

         Update            : b8c1 (#2)
         New Version       : 3.4.4
         Installed Version : 3.4.4

(15) [ ] eServer System x3755 BMC Update
         Severity          : Recommended
         Reboot            : Reboot Required to take effect
         Update ID         : ibm_fw_bmc_zybt42a_windows_i386
         New Version       : 1.05 (ZYBT42A)
         Installed Version : 1.05 (ZYBT42A)

(16) [*] MegaRAID 8480 SAS Controller Firmware
         Severity          : Recommended
         Reboot            : Reboot Required to take effect
         Update ID         : lsi_fw_megasas_1.03.00-0225_windows_32-64
         New Version       : 1.03.00-0225
         Installed Version : Undetected

Legend:
Type the item number to toggle selected [*] or not selected [ ]
Type 'a' to accept the menu
Type 'f' to select all entries
Type 'q' to quit without processing the entries
[1-16,a,q,f]>
```

to this (the GUI)...

Before, the command line interface had been accepted by users. Not a lot of people were questioning it. But with the command line, there was no way people would find mass appeal in churning out line commands just to do anything. Had the GUI not been adopted, the way we use computers today would be completely different, and who knows if they would have ever gotten their mass appeal.

Adoption of the GUI was one of Steve Jobs' biggest crusades during his first time running Apple. Even though the technology was already available, it was Jobs who knew what to do with it, and Xerox sat on it. You'll see throughout history that technology is either adopted or it is shelved. It was Jobs who made sure that the GUI was something that wasn't shelved. I can't imagine computers becoming such a mainstream phenomenon without it—and for that, I'm very thankful.

It's just jaw-dropping to think about how much faster data transfer speeds have gotten. I was churning out my first website on a 56K modem, and now I can blaze on one gigabit downloads. The higher the speeds, the more you can do, download, upload, and stream. Facebook wouldn't have been able to become one of the world's largest businesses without high-speed internet. Neither would Amazon, which currently owns 40 percent of servers on the common web (meaning anything indexed on search engines), or any of the other successful online businesses that such a diverse array of people have been able to start.

SO UNDER THE HOOD OF THE TECHNOLOGY, WHAT IS OUR ECONOMIC DNA?

I believe at the core of our economy's DNA lies the potential for *anyone* to create value and make money doing it. But that doesn't mean *everyone* can, and it certainly doesn't mean that everyone will.

Our economy's DNA is made up of obstacles, difficulties, and privileges that differ for each player. The entrepreneurs entering the game also come from many different starting points. Some have money they can invest from the beginning, while others have to fight for every dollar they earn. But no matter where your starting point on the board is, relative to the finish line, your potential to become a successful entrepreneur remains the same.

When it comes to our economy's DNA, we also think in terms of winners and losers. The winners' table in recent years would include the likes of Jeff Bezos, Bill Gates, and Mark Zuckerberg, to name a few. The list of those at the losers' table is much longer, but few people ever hear those names. That's partly because history itself is written for and by the winners and partly because aspiring entrepreneurs only want to hear about the success stories in which the embattled protagonist overcomes the odds and obstacles to be victorious. I think we all hope to imitate what they've done in our own way.

We even think of losing through the lens of the winners. We are obsessed with talking about the "early failures" of the great entrepreneurs of the age and how they overcame them. Don't get me wrong, this is important. Learning to accept and overcome failure is an integral part of becoming a successful entrepreneur, but there are many important lessons you can learn from the losers of this game who never made a comeback, too. Pay attention to them. You need to learn to lose in order to win. I believe many would-be entrepreneurs are scared off or intimidated by this dichotomy of winners and losers. They are too concerned with becoming the next Apple, rather than forming stable, viable businesses that provide real value to people. Put it this way: if you are running a company that provides gainful employment to a handful of individuals, including yourself, with a healthy surplus, income even larger than what you would earn in a stereotypical nine-to-five job, would that not be considered successful? To me, it would. But the news won't talk about you as a "winner," and you won't necessarily be offered a seat at the winners' table. But don't be fooled. You don't have to be a member of the elusive 1 percent to make an impact or to be considered a successful entrepreneur in my book (pun intended).

So if our economy offers the potential for anyone to create real value as an entrepreneur, why doesn't everyone do it? I think it's because many people are misguided in pursuing the right ideas in the wrong ways. They branch off onto the wrong path and never know how to recalibrate themselves for the rest of their lives, while pursuing distractions to feel better about themselves. Others, sadly, realize what they *could* have done too late. Some would-be entrepreneurs have jobs that are high-earning, so they don't want to give those up, even if the jobs serve no greater purpose. Some are too busy fighting every day to survive to ever think about entrepreneurship. Some just can't seem to overcome their own low self-esteem. I've met too many people who were overwhelmed by feeling the system was simply stacked against them and didn't try to do anything at all. No matter your circumstances, though, I'm still convinced that the secret to entrepreneurship is that *anyone* can do it and it can come from anywhere. The subjects of some of the best success stories overcame a lot to get where they are today—immigration to a new country, extreme poverty, tragic circumstance. Adversity is a great teacher, and when you have limited opportunities readily available to you, you have to get creative.

PHIL LIBIN AND THE POTENTIAL POWER OF GREAT TIMING

There is no greater force than timing. Your timing will determine the resources at your disposal to create your product, how people react to your product, and whether or not your product will be truly accepted in the market. Phil Libin, the cofounder and former CEO of Evernote, is an expert on timing. When Phil launched Evernote, his purpose was to create a second brain for people. But Phil also knew that Evernote would not have worked if it had launched during, say, the dot-com boom. Libin needed to wait until the world changed just enough so that the formerly impossible became hard to execute but not impossible to execute. When assessing whether or not a problem has gone from impossible to hard to solve, Libin suggests that you ask yourself these two questions:

1. What was impossible about it before?
2. What is *changing* now to make it possible?

Once you've determined the possibility of solving the problem, that still doesn't completely tell you if your timing is right. You need to answer *two more* questions:

1. Is your idea sufficiently important?
2. Why haven't other people done this yet if it's now possible?

According to Phil, if the idea seems too easy, it may already be too late to capitalize on it. Every new idea that you have, you need to run through this test—it really determines if you are going to succeed or fail.

Your exercise:

Run your own idea for a business through Phil Libin's litmus test.

Have you noticed any changes in the way that you perceive your idea? If you don't have any ideas of your own, analyze companies that are currently doing well. When did they start, and when did they really take off?

I REALLY LIKE TO STUDY THE PAST BECAUSE IT GIVES ME A LOT OF PERSPECTIVE FOR TODAY

It's a faraway memory, but in the colonial economy we were still considered "preindustrial." If you transported me back to this era, I would feel like I was on an alien planet. We are so far removed at this point from what it was like to run a business in colonial times. If you spoke of an "industrial revolution," people would look at you like you had two heads. As we go through the past, you'll see how, in many ways, it's still difficult to comprehend and predict the future from our current vantage point. Before the Industrial Revolution, most economies were hyperlocalized. Wagon transport was prohibitively expensive, and there was almost a total lack of roads connecting the colonies. And, of course, no trains yet. Economical distance for transporting low-value agricultural commodities was about twenty-five miles. *Think* about that for a second: *twenty-five miles*. Meanwhile, today, you could have something shipped across the world in a day. Think about that...

It really does give you some perspective of the vastly different lives we live today. And think about this: this isn't as long ago, historically, as it sounds. If the average person today lives to be about seventy-five years old, you're looking back at about three to four generations ago. That isn't very distant at all.

But many critical advancements were also made between the colonial era and today that were critical toward building a functioning society. From drinkable water to electricity to food production, there was going to be a ceiling for just how far people could go without technology. They wouldn't have been able to have as big a society as we do now, that's for sure.

I think that by looking back through these big moments, while you can't tell what exactly is going to happen tomorrow, you can acquire a perceptiveness to seeing how things evolve over time. You'll also be able to study just how much people's expectations have changed in quick spurts. Fifty years may seem like a while to you, but in the grand scheme of things, it's pretty short.

WITH HIGHER EXPECTATIONS COME BIGGER TECHNOLOGY AND RESPONSIBILITIES

You need to think about the aspects of your business besides what you are producing. *How* are you producing? Most customers today expect you to provide them with what they need instantaneously without them needing to be physically present. But they still want that personal connection—and they want to feel pride in the service and products they're buying from you.

Their tolerance for waiting on results or being told to jump through hoops to get something done is waning. There is a growing expectation for businesses to be able to read your mind and know your pain points and your perspective, all in an instant. Some people now have that default expectation that businesses already know in advance what they want. This extends to our growing expectations of how companies should present themselves. We now hold companies to the standards of their packaging, delivery process, and customer experience process.

During the 1950s, advertisers could get away with insulting the intelligence of their audience. But today's consumers want to be educated. There is a new level of sophistication. Customers want to be directly *involved* in the process of what they buy. They want to become a part of the operations.

There is no better example of this than how Johnny Earle runs Johnny Cupcakes. He's coined his methodology "experiential storytelling." Everything is thought out and crafted into the Johnny Cupcakes experience for his customers.

Let's take his clothing store, or should I say bakery, in Boston as an example. From the outside, you will swear it is a real bakery. When you walk in, you'll believe it. It smells like a bakery. You'll see the equipment found in any bakery, the branding that a bakery is there. But that is when you'll notice something strange: another door. Open that, and you'll stumble into a bakery with shirts, clothing, hats, and other merchandise for sale. Most of these goods are sold in refrigerators, on oven racks, and over oven tops.

This is an experience that the modern consumer doesn't forget. In fact, it is what makes his brand so influential. It grows organically through word of mouth: others sharing about the fact that they stumbled into a clothing store that was actually a bakery...a bakery that was actually a clothing store...an April Fool's prank that they couldn't believe was real!

Of course, Johnny backs this up with high-quality products. At a recent keynote, Johnny explained the power of making something others want to share, that every little detail matters when building a business in today's New Economy. He uses his to-go boxes as the perfect example. Paraphrasing from his talk:

> *Our to-go boxes at Johnny Cupcakes are designed to mimic what most bakeries use for pastries. We made sure the quality of these boxes is high enough, that*

customers do not want to throw them out but instead, store them in their house and show it off to their friends and family! Make it into a story. It grows the allure of Johnny Cupcakes, and without spending a single advertising dollar, I have managed to share our brand with new people who otherwise would have never heard of us prior!

People reveal a lot about themselves through their behavior—the recorded version of this behavior can be turned into true insights that can be applied over and over again. This is where data come in. The accumulation and analysis of that data nudge us closer to the truth, letting us feed back to the customer what they desire.

THROUGH THE TIMES THAT OLD INDUSTRIES DIE, NEW ONES WILL THRIVE

Joseph Schumpeter was an influential Austrian economist who, in 1942, coined the term "creative destruction." You've probably seen this unfold in your life many times. You can thank the exponential growth of technology for that one. One of the most famous examples of this is the story of Netflix and Blockbuster. Blockbuster, hard to believe, was once a staple in the average American household. It was common to spend a Friday night going to Blockbuster, returning your VHS from the previous week, and renting a new one for the weekend. What must have felt like magic, the invention of digital streaming mixed with more powerful computers and quicker household internet speeds, bred the rise of Netflix. Within only a few years of digital streaming being introduced by Netflix, Blockbuster filed for bankruptcy, and a new trend in user behavior was born as another died. Customers had a better, more convenient, and affordable business model available to them. There was no going back. Blockbuster failed to innovate and continue to compete.

Data are the new industry, and every entrepreneur has the opportunity to leverage data. There are many ways that entrepreneurs can approach this opportunity. Think about all of the companies and services that we take for granted today that less than twenty years ago weren't fathomable, such as the following:

- e-commerce
- Crowdfunding
- 3-D printing and manufacturing
- Sharing economy
- Online media companies
- Online dating
- Online advertising

WHAT'S MY PERSONAL MISSION THAT I SHARE WITH MANY AROUND THE WORLD?

I want to connect and empower people through technology and entrepreneurship. This is a colossal mission that is so much bigger than me.

Today, we have the most *efficient means of doing business that we have ever had.* Dependence on technology itself will usher in a slow phasing out of humanity's value to running the economy. But I still believe technology can be a tool for entrepreneurs to elevate humanity and help more people live happy and fulfilling lives. And as the New Economy continues to take ever-different shapes, the supply of tools will become all the greater.

We have a choice as entrepreneurs to enhance or change lives. I believe that businesses should exist to provide value in a solution to people's needs while being responsible for the next generation. This mission is more than just a way to feel good about your business. Finding your *position* in fulfilling this mission is part of finding your foothold in this New Economy. Without that, you're toast.

So what's my *position* in this economy?

I don't pretend to be curing cancer or saving lives, but I have had the opportunity to serve companies that want to build some great things for people. A lot of these companies have some ideas that could produce some watershed moments for humanity. But they don't have the digital infrastructure ready. That's my position and where I come in. By helping these people get their digital infrastructure ready and compete in today's New Economy, I get to serve many missions at once and have the privilege and honor of seeing these companies producing watershed moments in human history grow in real time. And by inspiring the next generation of entrepreneurs, I can be a part of a greater movement for the next breakthrough technologies, advancements, and services that better all of our lives.

IT CAN ALL FEEL SO OVERWHELMING—ALMOST LIKE IT'S ALL TOO MUCH

There is a reason why we cry and moan when we are on hold for an hour. There is a reason why we become flat-out pissed off when receiving an unexpected bill. There is a reason why we become annoyed if it takes days to hear back on a simple question. There is a reason why we become furious when getting the same runaround, treated as if we don't know better. It is because we expect businesses to do *more for us* in the New Economy.

This is no longer the exception; it is the norm. So have we become a society full of short-term-focused people, requiring constant gratification without putting in the extra legwork? Have we, as consumers, become ungrateful, greedy, and impatient? Sure we have, in some ways. The use of technology—whether on your phone, your computer, or any other device—has made a lot of people distracted and lazy. On the other hand, it gives us access to learn and do things that we could have never dreamed of. Furthermore, because we have the opportunity to instantly communicate with people from around the world, the possibilities are both truly wonderful and potentially catastrophic. The choice is yours. With devices being made to glue you in more and more, you'll need to become effective in discerning the distractions from the ways that technology can legitimately help you improve yourself.

IN ITS GREATEST POTENTIAL FORM, THE NEW ECONOMY ALLOWS US TO GET BACK TO A "PEOPLE FIRST" MINDSET

Everything I've spoken of so far is about making a better experience for the consumer.

1. Quicker response times
2. Building relationships
3. Taking time to understand needs deeply
4. Educating customers about what they're really getting
5. Saving time
6. Saving money

One of my biggest hopes for the New Economy is that there will be increasingly more opportunities for people to become closer once again. Small towns and cities used to be built around Main Streets. These places were the commercial and social "heart" where the bulk of people gathered. People today speak with so much nostalgia of Main Street, where shop owners would remember who you were, what you ordered, when you would come in, and even details about your family and your life. They'd grow up with you, see you change, and be a significant component of your own life from childhood through adulthood. It was the epitome of the doo-wop era!

I believe that Main Street mentality is coming back, and it's going to be better than ever. It's just packaged in a whole new way. Our technology augments the opportunity for these types of services to operate at economies of scale that they once couldn't. I love going to local bookstores around Philadelphia, where each new store I explore introduces new possibilities of books I never even knew I wanted to read.

I feel this same sense of adventure going into these bookstores as I did when I would dial up the 56K modem. But local bookstores had also been killed off by the big chains such as Borders (bankrupt) and Barnes & Noble (fine for now). And then, something interesting happened. Because local bookstores could also sell all of their products online as well as on site, they started to make a comeback. Local bookstores were a very unprofitable business only a decade or so ago due to high rents and lack of customers. But now that they can take advantage of the economies of scale that the internet provides, they can subsidize their local presence and still thrive. These bookstores can reach people outside of their local sphere of influence on social media to build and maintain great relationships with customers who are from anywhere, in addition to the locals—we can call, email, text, and chat with our customers without their being at the store themselves. We have the ability to automate such assets and make them available at the customer's disposal, 24-7.

Digital-only businesses, such as my company, Chop Dawg, can follow the same cornerstone beliefs that Main Street once had: putting the customer first. Remembering and caring about the customer. Not treating others like numbers but as individuals who matter. Being people first. The doo-wop era is back, repackaged, and ready to go. It is the New Economy that we all now partake in.

I've found so many more opportunities to be personal through digital technology. My team and I take this mentality to heart. Just because technology allows the possibility, we never hide behind our screens. With all these communication tools available to us, we have no excuse to ever let emails sit in our inboxes for long. We ensure that all of our clients have our personal email addresses and cell phone numbers. We intentionally get our clients involved in the process when we build their web and mobile applications and strive to educate them about why we are working on what. Technology is a great way to augment our services, but if we stripped all of that away, we would strive for the same level of care. We can build real relationships with meaning. We can make real, positive changes that leave the world better than what we started with.

THINK FOR A MOMENT ABOUT HOW DIFFICULT IT ONCE WAS TO START A NEW BUSINESS

In the past, most would-be entrepreneurs had to pay a colossal cost of entry to compete in this game. They either had to take out a loan or commit their savings in order to purchase a property (or take out a lease), buy the equipment needed, afford labor, and hope they could build something sustainable to last. If they failed, they were looking at their large loan to pay back without income, or else loss of their life savings. Daunting, right?

But for some people participating in the New Economy, the script has been flipped. While this is not the case for everyone, I had the ability to start a company really cheaply, and I never could have done this in any other era. I began Chop Dawg with a grand total of $10, which was used to purchase a domain name.

That's not to say that the point of entry can't cost a lot of money.

It really depends on what you're doing, but as technology standards rise, so do costs. Applications that we build for entrepreneurs can cost between $50,000 and $1,000,000. That sounds like a lot, but the entrepreneurs' recurring overhead is greatly reduced. These are one-time fixed costs that require little to no labor to maintain. Once their product is up, they have the ability to earn money with little to no expenses besides the server.

Small brick-and-mortar businesses, as well as digital businesses, have tools that must have seemed like science fiction years ago. Customer relationship managers can keep all of your customer data at your immediate disposal. Websites serve as 24-7 salespeople that don't require sales commissions. They offer the ability to sell your goods or services to anyone, anywhere, without being limited to just location. Personalized social media pages let you broadcast your own message to those who want to see it, without requiring an intermediary or permission, and start virtual communities built around your target audience. In the past, only the Goliaths could pay for such a luxury. Today, even for small brick-and-mortar locations, there is so much opportunity that just didn't exist years ago.

Few people know this better than Sam Hodges, who is the cofounder and US managing director of Funding Circle.

Originally, Sam was the owner of a successful chain of fitness gyms; he wanted to expand his business, but he'd been denied a loan more than *ninety-six* times from big banks. That's when he realized that the banking system was broken for small businesses. In response, he created his own marketplace where small business owners could borrow money directly from individual or institutional investors. As it turned out, there are plenty of people who would like to become individual investors with sustainable, revenue-generating small businesses with a mission they can get behind! In fact, there are quite a few competitors to Funding Circle today.

With each quality loan granted for a small business, Sam Hodges is chipping away at the previously unequitable lending system.

GETTING LEFT BEHIND IN THE WAVE

I can't help but recall my struggle back in 2009, trying to sell websites to small businesses that didn't want one. They had been fine for years before needing one, so why get one now?

Today, most of those businesses are long gone. They failed

to adapt to the New Economy. By the time having a website became the common wisdom, it was too late for a lot of them to get on the train.

Since my first time selling websites, it's astounding just how much has been created and the speed at which it's happened. We've gone, in a short time, from the creation of online communities, websites, and search engines, to everyone having a smart device in the palm of their hand. Smartphones, Alexas, Google Homes, smart watches, intelligent televisions, chatbots, emailing software, AI... the list goes on and on.

Without the technological tools to adapt to an economy that will eventually be run by machines, not humans, you will fail. But trust me, you won't be able to use the framework in this book to your benefit if you forgo the human qualities behind entrepreneurship. Success in the New Economy requires both.

CHAPTER 3

HOW TO USE THE ENTREPRENEUR'S FRAMEWORK

I want you to look up, away from this book for just a minute. Give it a good minute or two.

Look around the room you're in. If you're outside while reading this, even better!

I'd like for you to look around and take note of everything that is the color red. Really take your time with this. Look at every single thing that's red and take a mental note, no matter how large or how small.

Now I want you to close your eyes. Picture your immediate surroundings and think about everything you know about it. Describe it to yourself as if it's right before your eyes. Got your visual picture? Good.

While keeping your eyes closed, can you remember what in your surroundings is the color green?

Ah, you weren't expecting that, were you?

Because you were focusing on the color red the entire time, everything else is hard to remember, even if it's a pretty familiar scene to you. It's easy to miss something you weren't thinking to look for.

Our brain works much the same way in identifying new opportunities. For most of us, we're always laser-focused on something or another, but are we focused on the right thing? Are you so focused you're missing out on potential opportunities you previously didn't know existed? Think about how you were focusing on the color red when, in reality, the color green was right in front of you, too.

HAVE YOU HEARD OF THE TERM "WANTREPRENEUR"?

You'll often read negative connotations regarding the term "wantrepreneur." To me, wantrepreneurs *are* aspiring entrepreneurs. However, they are aspiring to become entrepreneurs for the *wrong* reasons. They aren't individuals driven to solve problems in the world and create value for others, or driven to make their own dent in the universe, no matter how big or how small. No, typically, they're motivated by the *idea* of being an entrepreneur versus the act of being an entrepreneur itself. The lifestyle, the money, the prestige of it—that is what a wantrepreneur is after. The success stories you often see in movies, newspapers, magazines, and on the internet portray entrepreneurs with such gusto that wantrepreneurs aspire purely to become the next story.

This isn't a book written to blame individuals for wanting that. I understand the pain that wantrepreneurs go through; I really do. It is ingrained in American pop culture to celebrate the successes of the top-performing entrepreneurs. It's taught in school that replicating the success of big individuals is what we should all strive for. It has become this icon for success in the eyes of most individuals. We see it with celebrities, on television, in the news. It looks so attainable to join this "elite" group, this way of life...Entrepreneurship can seem easy from a distance. You think, *Why can't it be me who joins into this elite group of stars, too?* Well, I fell into that same trap early in my entrepreneurial career.

Add on the fact that unlike something like, say, basketball, which has obvious standards for who has or lacks the talent (and physicality) necessary to become a professional, entrepreneurship doesn't present such physical boundaries. On the surface, it appears to be much more attainable. I can't tell you just by sitting in a room with some people who has the DNA to be a CEO of a startup versus someone who would fail spectacularly. There is no such physical attribute that allows us to identify that.

Therefore, almost anyone can be fooled into thinking entrepreneurship is automatically the lifestyle for them. What it takes time to realize is that the true entrepreneurs have naturally gifted talents equivalent to those of professional athletes, dancers, engineers, and other top performers in industries around the globe, which are impossible to replicate. It does not matter how smart you are, how cunning you are, how charismatic you are. The best entrepreneurs have a special part of their personal DNA that is different from the rest.

Most people diving into the world of entrepreneurship often read about the Mark Zuckerbergs, Steve Jobses, John Rockefellers, Elon Musks, and Arianna Huffingtons of the world. They dig into the stories about companies like Slack raising more than $427 million in investor funds and valued at more than $2 billion (this is true). They're fed an inspiring story about a company they've never heard of that started less than three years ago and was recently acquired for more than $500 million in cash.

As you start to realize what is in the news, what is discussed, and what is shared in pop culture about what entrepreneurs do for a living, it makes a lot of sense how wantrepreneurs are bred. And I think I know why it looks so attainable.

Entrepreneurship sounds and appears lucrative. It seems like what separates you from the success stories you've seen in movies is nothing but doing it yourself. Except, if you're reading this book, you know this isn't the case. Not in the slightest.

The reality is that most entrepreneurs are the ones who own small shops across Main Street, run small enterprises, or have an app available on the phone that earns a few thousand dollars a month, the ones who provide a service that most people need and that they can provide to your local community. Most entrepreneurs are making enough to make ends meet, to support their families, their team, and their customers, and are not earning millions (or billions)...and that is more than good enough. You don't need to make it so big. Big entrepreneurship is just what's talked about.

One of my favorite things to do when I speak at universities and colleges is to ask the audience, "How many of you would love to earn $100,000 a year?" Everyone raises their hands, of course!

One hundred thousand dollars a year. That is much more money than the average American salary at this time. Yet, for most who are feeding into the media machine with their pop culture expectations of entrepreneurship, that doesn't sound like enough money. The thought doesn't even cross their minds that $100,000 could very much be the definition of success if you're doing what you love. If you can build a business that makes that much of an impact, that earns you money for doing what you love, isn't that something remarkable on its own?

Wantrepreneurs not only are at a disadvantage because they focus on the wrong things, but they also have a warped perspective of what success should be. Success isn't being the founder of a billion-dollar company. Success is building something of substance, of value, that earns you a legitimate income doing what you love. That might not be *sexy* to the media or pop culture, but who cares, as long as it's still lucrative and, more importantly, so much more attainable for you and me?

In reality, the first steps of starting a business happen through good old-fashioned experimentation. It's a slow burn. You need to have a curious mindset so that you really have the desire and motivation to put in the work. It's really about questioning how things work. Do you know of the scientific method? I remember learning the scientific method in class back in high school. It was one of the few things that interested me in school because it exposed me to my first framework for the way I think.

You see, the scientific method is a framework for acquiring knowledge that many scientists have been using since about the seventeenth century. It's deceptively simple as a model, and it's formed the basis of scientific thinking and experimentation for the past few hundred years. This very method of acquiring knowledge has helped foster some of the most mind-bending discoveries of all time. I also strongly believe that the scientific method can be applied to entrepreneurship, and I think about this on an almost-daily basis.

Here's the scientific method:

1. Make observations
2. Think of questions of interest
3. *Formulate hypotheses*
4. Develop testable predictions
5. Gather data to test predictions
6. Refine, alter, expand, or reject hypotheses
7. Develop general theories
8. *And it circles back*

Doesn't this sound like the early stages of what a curious and observant entrepreneur might go through to start a new business, to build a new product, or to introduce a new service to the world? And it's not just for the early stages. I also consider the scientific method when I run into new problems and curiosities. Like I said, in one way or another I think about the scientific method almost daily.

Benjamin Franklin (my entrepreneurial idol) is the embodiment of the curious and observant mind. He questioned how things work throughout his entire lifetime. When making discoveries, he never got too caught up in the process of *why* things worked exactly, but he was constantly focused on the *how*. This way of thinking really helped him discover a lot of things for humanity. One wonders what a man with his intelligence and curiosity could have accomplished if he had today's digital resources at his disposal.

Did you know that back in Benjamin Franklin's day, people didn't know that lightning was electricity? Lightning was widely accepted as the "wrath of God," capable of smiting evildoers. Fire spreading and destroying homes was a huge concern back then because most homes were made out of wood. One lightning strike could destroy entire blocks of homes.

Benjamin questioned this assumption and employed the scientific method.

Through a series of experiments, he found evidence that

lightning and electricity were of the same phenomenon. His famous kite experiment in Philadelphia in June 1752 (although this exact date is debated) was the pinnacle of proving that lightning and electricity were the same thing. Ever the practical entrepreneur, Benjamin then sold lightning rods that people could put on the top of their houses to protect their wooden homes from fires. He used his findings to create something that truly solved a problem for all.

SADLY, I DON'T SEE THE SPIRIT OF BENJAMIN FRANKLIN IN THE MANY WANTREPRENEURS

Wantrepreneurs tend to fall for the path of copying others' work. It happened after Groupon and Uber showed signs of massive growth. All of the copycats came in, saw some minor successes (some even saw some big temporary wins), then fought for the scraps, and now have vanished. But why?

Michael Gasiorek (the codirector of the San Francisco chapter of Startup Grind) once referred to this tendency as the "calling of the herd." Something successful comes along seemingly overnight, and the herd forms because other people want to experience that same success.

What the wantrepreneurs are missing through this calling of the herd is the opportunity to work in much more profitable industries they don't know or think about. For example, the elder care industry is something that is going to keep growing, but I don't know of any wantrepreneurs who want to create things that service senior citizens. The elder care industry just doesn't have that same flashy glow that the herd craves. And that's such a mistake. Think about all of the baby boomers hitting their senior years!

Michael pointed me toward a company in the elder care industry called GoGoGrandparent, which is a human AI interface layer for apps like Uber. Rather than the senior citizen having to schedule pickups themselves on the Uber app, the AI interface will do all of the arranging for them. All they need to do is get into the car; everything else has been taken care of. Imagine having a grandchild for hire!

The possibilities of how we can serve our elderly are pretty endless in my mind, and the market will only keep growing. I hope to see more entrepreneurs enter this space. OK, so finding practical and effective ideas based on real needs is definitely something that is very possible. So why aren't more entrepreneurs biting into ideas like this?

Michael said it's likely because more ideas are built on privilege rather than true needs.

> *"Too many apps are being built by white male engineers who live in San Francisco to do things that their mommy used to do. You may build a company that is*

financially valuable, but will you be remembered? Tech
should not be serving the privileged classes. It should be
building a better world."

I also think that by becoming part of the herd, you actually are committing yourself to a more boring career. Without originality in yourself or your life, you don't stand out in the crowd of people who want to do the same thing as you do. With some originality, you truly will, I promise.

Michael made a good point to me about what entrepreneurs lacking in originality are missing out on:

"How sexy is it to be another attractive person at the
bar? You are just another one of the pack. You don't have
any other desire besides being part of the pack. You are
more concerned with appearing like the coolest one in
the room."

When you're part of the herd, you let go of the opportunity for distinction. Unfortunately, the herd is big, and many people are trying to replicate the same magic that the unicorns have created for themselves.

SO WHY DOES IT SEEM LIKE SO MANY PEOPLE WANT TO BE PART OF THE HERD?

Without a doubt, fear keeps the wantrepreneur from

finding out what they don't want to know. If they're going to put in the work, shouldn't the outcome be guaranteed to be a good one? They don't even want to imagine that failure could be in the cards. In reality, though, entrepreneurs experiment all of the time and fail on many things before landing on something that could be a success. To the wantrepreneur, that seems like a grind. The entrepreneur figures out how to give something their best shot.

Many people in life also go through the same educational framework: graduate from high school, take out a large loan for school, graduate from college, and then get a job and pay off that student loan debt. But here's the thing: this educational framework is just one option that you have.

It's also not the only way you can learn how to start a business or get a job. Not even close. In reality, if there's one thing being an entrepreneur has taught me, it is that no two people learn in the same way. So many people learn in different, unique ways. Yet through traditional schooling, I see an attempt at a one-size-fits-all approach to education (although I do hope that, one day, technology will change this). It's the building of the herd mentality when you think about it, which is another reason why the "calling of the herd" producing big numbers makes sense to me. Today, many entrepreneurs ascribe to the Silicon Valley-style of entrepreneurship in a similar way.

In contrast, true non-herd entrepreneurship requires you forging your own path, which can be uncomfortable, especially because you may not even know how you learn best yet. You may also lack the objectivity and supportive community to find the best learning path for yourself.

I asked my friend Christie Pitts, general partner of the Backstage Capital investment firm, about how entrepreneurs can become more objective. Before Christie joined Backstage Capital, she served as Verizon Ventures' development manager.

Christie told me:

> "A great way to attain objectivity is to consider multiple perspectives. It's important for entrepreneurs to have a circle of people whom they trust and who can provide them with honest and candid feedback."

Finding the thing that is just right for you is, I hate to say, pure trial and error. This trial-and-error process becomes so much easier when you have a circle of people who can give you sound advice, help you become more objective, and act as your mentors along the way.

You're probably not going to want to stick with the first opportunity that you've identified for yourself. I mean, look at me as an example. I started Chop Dawg as a website design company (more as a website design freelancer in the traditional sense) before it became the technology partner and app development agency that it is today. But when you identify a new opportunity that later turns out to be much better, your wiser self will thank your past self for not settling on anything. What makes this process fun is the natural desire to learn about how things in the world work.

I think it's the lure of getting caught in the idea high that stumps wantrepreneurs the most. They don't want to figure out how to prove their concept and instead keep cuddling up with their assumptions.

That leads to failure.

So before you go all in on your next idea, ask yourself these questions:

1. Are you willing to risk further failure and sacrifice money?
2. Are you willing to put the work into validating a new assumption?
3. Figure out what's missing—why was your original assumption not validated, and why didn't your idea work?
4. Can you do all of this quickly so you can keep going or move on?

Find your answers to these questions. You need them to make your ideas a reality. Once you've thought this through, go all in and immerse yourself in this new idea for as long as it takes you to figure out whether you should go to the next step or just move on. Know that along the way, you'll deal with the fear of loss, rejection, destitution, embarrassment, you name it.

Entrepreneurship truly is about the journey and not just the destination.

THIS PHILOSOPHY ALSO APPLIES WHEN SEEKING INVESTORS

Don't just ask for investment right away. In fact, you don't need to ask for an investment at all in order to get offers.

I recently had the pleasure of speaking to Phil Kennard about this very topic. He is the cofounder and CEO of Futurestay.

Futurestay is used by thousands of people who rent out their vacation homes to guests. Its technology automates dozens of interactions, including payments, emails, inquiries, and any refunds or cancellations that may occur between booking and checkout for vacation rental entrepreneurs. They're serving a new market of rental entrepreneurs who use third-party booking platforms, such as Airbnb, Booking.com, and HomeAway, to book their guests. These are individuals running professional full-scale operations and making serious money doing it. Futurestay handles all of the complications unique to each of these third-party platforms and merges the operations of vacation rental entrepreneurs all into one convenient place.

Futurestay has raised more than $4 million and has been really scaling up its technology. Talk to Phil and you'll see why it has been able to raise so much. He's an expert in his industry, and he and his cofounder, Jon Fabio, were early to the vacation rental industry party and ready to rock.

When it comes to getting funds, here's what he has learned:

"If you seek investment, you will get advice. If you seek advice, you may get an investment."

Phil and Jon started out by pitching Futurestay at local entrepreneurship meetups but not in order to raise money. What they *wanted* was feedback. When they gave their first pitch to potential investors there, they were eviscerated in the Q&A and had to answer some very tough questions.

But that was OK with them—they answered each one of their questions with gusto and took all of their feedback graciously. And then something interesting happened.

The next day, Phil and Jon received an email from the

investors saying they were very *impressed* by the presentation. But why the harsh criticism the day before? Part of it was that they were being tested—what the investors had loved about Phil and Jon was their willingness to take criticism. They could really see the founders' intrinsic desire to listen and really soak in advice.

According to Phil, investors fully realize that your business will evolve and shift over time. In fact, the investors want to see that same realization in the founders that they back. They want to know you are adaptable. Whatever you sell on day one isn't likely what you will be selling a few years from now.

Investors want to see how willing you are to embrace change—that starts with an openness to feedback, rather than becoming defensive. I see many entrepreneurs struggling with an intractable attachment to their mission, which causes them to miss out on other, better opportunities. Sometimes the mission needs to be adjusted and changed in order to work. Take Groupon, for example.

SOME ENTREPRENEURS HAVE DIFFICULTY OVERCOMING AN ATTACHMENT TO THE ORIGINAL MISSION

Andrew Mason, the founder of Groupon, was really committed to sticking to his original mission in the early days. In fact, these early days were before it was even Groupon at all. In 2007, the company we now know as Groupon launched as The Point. It was a social media platform that gathered groups of people together to collectively solve problems and raise money. In one of the more outlandish groups, users banded together to try to make Chicago a warmer place year-round, and collectively raised funds to place a dome over the city in the winter months. In case you haven't been to Chicago recently, I can assure you that didn't end up happening. Of course, the vast majority of groups that got together on The Point got some really practical things done together; there was a community forming.

But investors felt there was an existential crisis afoot when it came to The Point's revenues. The Point was never meant to make a lot of money, and a lot of the development team was OK with that. But by 2008, it was clear that The Point wasn't making enough money or getting enough interest to stay viable in the eyes of its financial backers.

What's interesting is, the initial business plan for The Point that cofounder Eric Lefkofsky had suggested *was* group buying as a way to make money. His proposal was based on a campaign that had been undertaken by a few users on the platform, which rounded up twenty or so people to buy the same product so they could get a group discount. To Eric, this was where the biggest potential for monetization lay.

But Andrew and the early team balked at that idea: "It doesn't fit with the mission."

They stuck with their original mission until the 2008 economic crash. With mounting pressure from investors to start generating real revenue, Andrew and his team relented and pursued a different mission of group buying. While there was a lot that needed to be done to make this transition successful, such as changing the business plan and the platform's mechanics, mitigating the impact on existing users, and attracting a fresh audience based on new development, the new mission's success had already been proven by users with that campaign on The Point.

WITH FUTURESTAY, PHIL AND JON CONTINUED TO DEFINE AND ADJUST THEIR MISSION AS NEEDED WHEN PITCHING

They focused on excelling at the small things, such as learning from customer complaints and improving user acquisition and retention. Meanwhile, each presentation they gave to investors explained the Futurestay mission more clearly. Each presentation integrated the feedback from the one that had come before. Their selling points were better told, and they were making real revenue to boot.

From the end of 2012 to the end of 2014, they pitched and pitched before inking a deal for their first $500,000.

Phil recalled:

"Pitches became so easy once the business itself became more sellable."

Another thing that wantrepreneurs hope is that raising money will solve all their problems. But there are so many things you can do without raising money. And investors want to see that you are viable as a company and can make money without them.

Phil always asked himself this question when he and Jon were courting investors:

"Have I done everything that I could for my business without raising money?"

They knew that investors wanted to see their resourcefulness. They needed to show investors that they were willing to do the legwork in getting their company profitable. What investors didn't want to see were excuses of why they hadn't done something simple, something they could do without their investment.

They had the advantage of being able to prove they were making money. Once they made a deal with Wix to offer Futurestay as a plug-in on their service, it became a real revenue generator. They were onto something, and the investors were ready.

Investors want to hop on a train that is already moving. I've seen too many wantrepreneurs with an aversion to being proven wrong, so they don't seek out proof of concept and instead pitch a lot of speculation to investors.

I HAVE FOUND THAT THE TIME SPENT IN FEAR OF BEING PROVEN WRONG IS WAY MORE PAINFUL THAN STAYING FROZEN (YET COMFORTABLE)

I've come to terms with the fact that fear, failure, and rejection are just part of the game. When you're just getting started with the framework, it can be difficult to get out of your comfort zone. What feels comfortable now can later lead to regret.

So instead of fearing the outcomes that risk hurting my pride or leaving me feeling really sad, I now possess a *fear of inaction*. To me, the regret of doing nothing is much worse than failure. I literally spend my time fearing how much regret I'm going to feel if I don't follow through with what I want to do.

It gives me such a feeling of inadequacy that it really helps stave off procrastination in a perverse sort of way. For this to work, though, you really need to commit yourself to the task at hand. If I didn't have a laser focus when starting Chop Dawg, I would have never written this book. Similar to the exercise that began this chapter, anything unrelated to Chop Dawg simply wasn't in my line of sight; it would only serve as a distraction from the real prize, from my ambition. Chop Dawg was my sole focus.

Sometimes I wonder why it is so hard for so many people to get started and commit to one idea the whole way through.

I've thought of a few possibilities that I feel really prevent people from following through on their ideas:

1. Fear of failure and everything that comes with it: losing money, personal rejection, and ultimately, embarrassment. My advantage was, of course, that I experienced failure later on without fearing it first. But many people are in fear of failure before they even get started, and that's hard.
2. Lack of personal identity. If you don't have a strong sense of who you are and what you really want, it's tough to get started and stand out. If you only seek to replicate others rather than doing your own thing, that'll also mess with your sense of control in the long run. If you don't believe that you have control of anything in your life, while also being afraid of anything you don't control, entrepreneurship will be tough.

does go the longest way of all. You just need to be real with yourself and your aspirations. I'll dive deeper into this in chapter 4 of the book.

I think that examining how you spend your free time is so important. Are you *really* happy with the way you spend your time? Have you identified an opportunity that you feel like you can't afford to be a part of?

Your exercise:

If you allocated the number of hours per day that you spend on yourself versus how much you spend on others' time, what would it be? Because you sleep (or should be sleeping, hopefully) for eight hours per night, subtract that from the twenty-four-hour total, working with a sixteen-hour total.

- How much time each day do you willingly give your time to someone else?
- How much time each day do you unwillingly give your time to someone else?
- How much time each day do you willingly or unwillingly waste by procrastinating?
- How much time each day do you spend commuting?
- How much time do you have for yourself?
- How much of your time do you feel was spent well?

Once you come up with these blocks of time, multiply

by seven, then by fifty-two. You'll get a general sense of how much time you have to yourself and how much value you're getting out of your own time. You'll get a sense of how much more of your life you can control than what you currently believe.

Once you run these figures, you may look at the results with regret.

Better you know, though! You may find that you've spent your time carelessly and aren't satisfied with what you've done. But isn't there opportunity after regret? Yes, there is.

BUILDING UP TO GRATITUDE

I consider there to be two types of gratitude:

- Gratitude for things in your life
- Gratitude for the things that don't directly involve you but do shape your daily existence

Let's focus on being grateful for the things in your life first, as I think that being at peace with yourself opens you up to the rest of the world, so to speak. Thinking about your advantages is a great first step to becoming more grateful in your life. Thinking about my own advantages has made me more humble as well.

4. Locating my first clie res. I have ended up with

5. Being recommended rm outcomes through my
    services   s. I'm going to use the per-

6. The media talking ab e back what led me to my

7. Building a team of tal book right now.
    Dawg

8. Turning Chop Dawg i seem easier for me to be

9. Becoming unsatisfie se I'm already happy with
    design and discover he thing: I'm happy with
    focus) for building ap ture self isn't any better

10. Pivoting from Chop D I'll be disappointed. I'm
    Subtle   so grateful for being where

11. Failing with Subtle o l.

12. Rebuilding Chop Da
    knowledge and know self—what led you to this
    and desire to become any perceived failures you

13. Working with my tea Hey, because I failed there,

14. Spending years on my
    building Chop Dawg t

15. Being told by colleag events led you to this very
    sionals in my field to this page of *The Entrepre-*
    for others to learn fro backward to two years ago,

16. Deciding to write this ld you have done *this* with-

17. Having the team to he

18. Rewriting this book t
    ensure it is flawless itude when we are stressed.
                          e more we focus on what
    Mapping out a personal rable, and anxious. We get

anxious over what we feel like we can't control. We fear that we will be exposed as frauds or miss the boat on something entirely. Some people even stress about having too much stress!

It all comes back to how you frame it to yourself. What is your go-to reaction right now when you're hit with stress? Do you feel like a victim of your situation, or do you know that you can overcome it?

Think back to the exercise of focusing on one color and leaving out everything else around it. So many of us get focused on the negative side of things going on in our lives and neglect to see the positives we should be proud of.

Choose to look for those positives, especially when times are tough. These are the things to hang on to, match your actions to, and push yourself toward.

NOW THINK ABOUT THE OTHER KIND OF GRATITUDE

The gratitude that's for the things that don't directly involve you personally but do shape your daily existence. Remember, you're *living in* the modern-day gold rush. Thanks to the advance of technology, it's technically easier to get started on something than ever before. You could easily play a part in the revolution yourself. Isn't that something to be grateful for? I cannot emphasize enough that the whole Entrepreneur's Framework is moot without gratitude.

When people hear the words "innovation" and "progress," they think of significant, quantifiable leaps. But I also encourage you to really appreciate what those leaps mean. Appreciate the fact that previous generations of your own family faced hardships to get to where your family is today. Appreciate the thousands and millions of lives before you who pushed the envelope in society, business, and technology to grant you the marketplace and opportunities that you now have. Appreciate the opportunities that their perseverance now presents to you. Being able to be an entrepreneur, in many cases, is a privilege.

"Gratitude is a practice, a habit, and a way of inhabiting your life, your world, and your days. It is, for me, a form of seeing. Gratitude is most of all the practice of fullness for me—it's seeing a wholeness embedded into the fabric of life. It encompasses loneliness and loss, terror, and fear. It does not deny life's hardships but brings them into fullness. To not be grateful is to not see that we are gifted with bodies that breathe to experience this life."

That was said by Gayle Karen Young, who used to be the chief talent officer at the Wikimedia Foundation. She's absolutely right—gratitude encompasses everything. You can't be grateful only when you're winning.

If you realize all of this and it all makes sense to you, I believe you could have the *chance* to become the entrepreneur that you're meant to be. When you first wake up in the morning and when you go to sleep at night, remind yourself of your own life's journey up to this point.

Think about everything that is and isn't in your control that grants you the privilege of being alive in this very moment, doing what you're doing. Take time to comprehend how much in human history, and your family history, has led you to this very moment. Take the good and bad, and really think about how they connect. And most of all, fall in love with the journey.

It's only in hindsight that I know that gratitude saved my butt back when we failed Subtle. I never questioned being an entrepreneur, and I'm grateful for my gratitude back then. I knew that I had screwed up, but that was such a pivotal moment for me. This moment of hard failure was when I realized that there had to be a *better* way to be an entrepreneur. I'm grateful I got shaken in that direction.

SO THAT'S MY WHY. THE NEXT SECTION OF THIS BOOK WILL BE ABOUT MY HOW

Next, I'll be going into each of the eight principles that make up the Entrepreneur's Framework. Each of these interconnected principles (*self-awareness, empathy, lead-*

ership, short-term thinking, long-term thinking, economics, operations, and *purpose*) will contain stories, lessons, history, interviews, and even actionable steps for you to put into action for your own business.

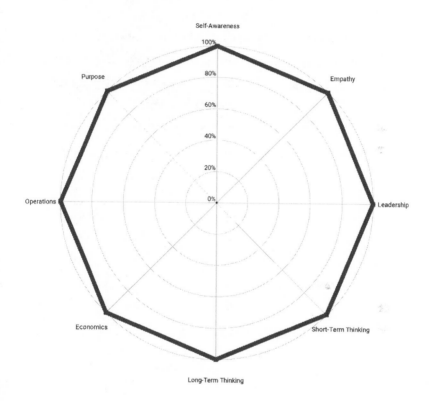

In the coming chapters, we'll dive in together on how to use this chart to assess yourself on how you're performing to each of the eight principles of the framework. Where do you need to improve?

The why we've been exploring serves as a Rosetta stone to everything you're about to read. Think back on my basketball example—you've now upped your entrepreneurial IQ, and it is time to learn how to play the game itself.

I'll be the first to say it's not easy. Setbacks and new challenges will appear. That is entrepreneurship 101. But with an inquisitive mindset and a perspective of gratitude, you'll be able to put the framework into action. You'll be able to handle the good times and the bad ones.

Section II

HOW

CHAPTER 4

SELF-AWARENESS

It was near the end of August 2013 when the weight of working nonstop for the past eight months while having nothing to show for it caused my brain to collapse in on itself. I had barely slept in weeks. Whenever I lay in bed, my mind would immediately be off to the races, question after question looping around in my brain.

- *Why am I in this mess?*
- *Am I letting down everyone who cares about me?*
- *How in the world could I have wasted $50,000, every dollar I had saved to this point?*
- *What have I done to my team? What will my family, friends, and colleagues think of me?*
- *How have I become a failure? I'm just one of the failures now.*

Back when we were churning out websites for small businesses, we had found some neat ways to enhance our service and make our own jobs easier. Our clients across the board had expressed the need to manage their websites without having to go through a steep learning curve. So we built our own tools in-house so our clients could easily maintain their sites on their own. We called these tools Odysseus (our website editor), Poseidon (our email client), and Genesis (our little digital cloud storage).

Not only did our clients love them, but these tools also allowed us to make a bit of recurring revenue through monthly access fees. So I did realize that there *could* be a demand for these services outside of our current clients. And of course with Odysseus, Poseidon, and Genesis, we already had a solution that was *completely validated* by our clients. So we were sure that other small businesses would want these same tools to manage their own sites.

BUT I HAD JUST RECENTLY COMMITTED OUR TEAM TO PIVOT FROM BUILDING SMALL BUSINESS WEBSITES TO BUILDING FULL-SCALE APPS

For that reason, I made sure that the idea of releasing our client tools to the public wasn't even considered. All I wanted was for us to move forward on building full-scale apps. It really was my way or the highway, and I was intractable on that.

I sensed that the demand for apps was going to skyrocket, but what I didn't understand was how much more difficult it would be to get a customer. I also didn't realize how bad our original branding was and that it didn't translate well with people who were paying top dollar to have an app built. At first glance, I'm sure people looking through our website thought we were just a bunch of kids who didn't really know how to do anything. These people were spending serious money on apps, and we were just some scruffy kids who were still known for building small business websites. These early struggles harkened back to when I was going door to door, except this time, I didn't even know how to approach anyone.

So, eventually, we thought, why wait for the dream client to come in when we could just build our own app and become our own dream client? Screw the people who didn't want us; we were going to enter the gold rush ourselves. We could be our own unicorns that were hitting the news and become household names. We already had the necessary tools to build this on our own; all we had to do was get out to market. That, we assumed, would be easy. Subtle would encompass all of the apps we believed *any* business would need to run their operations online:

- Manage their storage on the cloud
- Be able to read their email on the same app
- Update their website in real time

- Blend the calendar and a customer relationship management (CRM) into one seamless tool
- Newsletter marketing management, content management, analytics, and social media management
- Handle customer service

Sounds like a lot, right? Today, combining these tools might seem like common sense. But back then, there was no all-in-one solution. (Slack wasn't a thing yet. Google Drive wasn't a thing yet. Google Analytics was just starting to become the norm. Buffer was brand new. Salesforce wasn't the dominant market force it currently is. WordPress wasn't nearly as popular as it is today.) Every app required a separate application, along with a new monthly fee, new setup, new training, and a learning curve.

We *did* have the foresight to identify that gap and the opportunity that many businesses, small and large, could benefit from. We wanted businesses' operations to feel "subtle." We began work on January 1, 2013, with a goal date of having this app launched by August 1. I had budgeted the $50,000 to last us all the way until that date, which we thought would be more than doable. And for the first few months, it was nothing but excitement and euphoria. We felt like adventurers, exploring a brand-new world. As a team, we had become closer than ever before, spending nearly every waking moment working on Subtle.

BY THE BEGINNING OF THAT SPRING, WE HAD ANNOUNCED TO THE WORLD WHAT WE HAD SPENT THE LAST SEVERAL MONTHS ON

Because we had nothing to actually show by this point, we technically marketed nothing. But we found out that didn't really matter. We still managed to get people excited on Twitter by telling vague ideas of what they could be signing up for. People didn't need to know what they were getting; they just wanted to know that they were going to be a part of the "future of work." Remember, this was 2013—marketing on Twitter was easy then, if you could generate some excitement and retweets. We learned that it was pretty easy to get people hyped up on little more than an idea.

Then we showed off some screenshots, and that really got people going—it gave the impression that the app was a real thing, that it was about to become something real and impactful. A few thousand people joined our waiting list. This only motivated us further—I mean, if thousands were already clamoring for just a *general* idea of what we had envisioned, how would they respond when they got to use the real thing?

BUT BY THE BEGINNING OF SUMMER, OUR ENTHUSIASM WAS BEGINNING TO FADE

Despite the hype and the sign-ups, we were growing frustrated with ourselves and one another. Even though we were working ourselves to death, we still were not maintaining the pace needed to finish by the deadline. We had spent a lot of time producing nothing that was usable at all.

And of course, up to this point, we had all but neglected Chop Dawg. We didn't shut it down, but we weren't marketing it either. Our complete and full attention was on Subtle. While it's good that we didn't outright abandon Chop Dawg, we were severely limiting our exit strategy in case Subtle failed, because our bread and butter had become a shell of its former self.

Honestly, we were spreading our priorities way too thin. We were effectively making six apps in one. The developers, who didn't have a clear road map of the app's design, were becoming infuriated with the designers because they kept working on things that were already in the middle of programming. The designers were becoming frustrated with development, as they wanted the product to look its absolute best and did not want to settle for anything less. It felt like we were trying to hit a moving target while blindfolded. Meanwhile, I was boiling inside because nothing was on schedule, the designs kept changing, and the app barely worked. I felt like I could not coordinate these two teams at all and that no one was making the effort that I wanted and expected them to. A few features were programmed and working, but we weren't even close to having a functioning app that could be released.

Throughout the entire Subtle era, our remote team would get together in person once a month to work "hackathon style." For those of you who aren't familiar with the hackathon concept, we would get together in a room to all focus on the same objective, such as completing a new feature, for an entire weekend, with almost zero breaks. We would not allow one another to leave until all of our tasks were completed. By August, we all hated these hackathons. They had instead become the entrepreneurial equivalent of a WWE cage-match ring.

THEN CAME ONE LAST HACKATHON. WE WERE GOING TO FINISH SUBTLE, NO MATTER WHAT

As usual, we all got together, but this time, we didn't know when our hackathon was going to end. I told everyone that our objective was to get this done and that no one was to walk out the door until it was ready, no exceptions. I was out of money, and in my mind, every minute that Subtle wasn't ready meant a higher chance of our having to pull the plug. I could not admit failure and give my team I had fully paid an excuse to bail. So anytime the team stopped working, even for a moment, I'd snap at them.

How did they not understand there was no time to waste? Why did no one feel the urgency that I did?

We all used to joke and have fun during these hackathons

in the early months of building Subtle, but now we just worked together in silence. For hours, everyone stared at their laptop screens, typing away while listening to music through their headphones. Finally, one of the team members "spoke out of line" and suggested we should grab a bite to eat. It was getting late, and no one had eaten the entire day. And just like that, my fuse went off. Oh, the *gall* to suggest that we break away for even a minute when we were down to the wire!

I lost complete control of my emotions. This is the moment when the reality of the situation hit me cold—my team had failed *me*, and I let them have it. I couldn't stop yelling at everyone in the room. And my tirade was the last straw for the team, too—they weren't going to put up with my abuse. So they left to eat without me. I had created a mutiny, and I was left there to think about how screwed we were. I sat in the bathroom for two hours and cried. I had no idea what to do. I felt powerless, like I had lost complete control. How could I have trusted this team, *my* team, with my money?

Once the team returned from dinner, two of them asked to speak to me privately. They explained to me they were tired of my treatment of them. They "weren't being paid enough to deal with this." They then blurted out the words that I knew were coming but never wanted to hear. It was time to *pull the plug* on Subtle.

That was it. Subtle was never going to launch because I had no team to do it. Instead, they had the *audacity* to tell me, after I had spent every dollar I had on them, that they weren't being paid enough? At least they got paid! What about me? What was just a waste of time for them was life-changing for me.

I wanted to fight the team on this. I *really wanted* to tell them off. But my rage finally cooled down during my four-and-a-half-hour drive back home. I realized that I really had nothing else to say. Everything that I had been doing for the past eight to nine months was wiped clean—nothing to show for it, all the money gone, and my team hated me. I couldn't begin to imagine what I was going to do now.

BELIEVE IT OR NOT, TODAY I DON'T CONSIDER THIS A LOSS BUT A NECESSARY LEARNING EXPERIENCE

I didn't know it at the time, but this pain was something I needed to go through to learn some valuable lessons. Without the failure of Subtle, I wouldn't have known about any of my flaws—flaws that would have eventually killed Chop Dawg, too. It also taught everyone on my team a valuable lesson—that we weren't acting like a team at all but instead a group of people in their own individual bubbles. We knew how to code and design apps, but we were incapable of making anything into a coherent whole. Subtle actually ended up being a practice canvas that we were able to screw up on, rather than making those mistakes while blowing someone else's money.

In retrospect, there were many reasons why we failed, namely:

1. No one had been in sync with anything from start to finish. We made things way too complicated for ourselves by constantly redoing designs and never agreeing on how the app should really work. We would work on one variation during a given week and then would be chasing a new idea the next. I also never adjusted our schedule, even as we were falling behind. We failed at Subtle because we were always working on a moving target, increasing our expectations and workload, but not adjusting for the date it would take to get there.

2. We should have built the *leanest* product possible to get it out the door. People were signing up for a product that they had a vague idea about; we could have and should have come out with a piece of the app. They would have been happy as long as they knew that they were getting the first iteration. It would have been much more cost-effective, and I could have spread my $50,000 budget rather than blowing it up. Instead, these would-be users just became angry that we never launched anything at all.

I wish I had known Phil Kennard during my Subtle

days, because I could have really learned about the right approach to building a minimum viable product (MVP) right then and there.

Phil was a software developer by trade, which meant he could tinker around with building a product himself. That made things a lot more flexible. He could quickly churn out an MVP and see what happened. It didn't need to be a final product, but it did need to honor a specific goal: to give the vacation-rental owner a home base to run everything from one place. Note that the goal of the MVP was not the same as the goal of Futurestay today, which is to provide vacation-rental owners with automated instant booking. For the MVP, there was no automation. Instead, it was meant to be a simple home base and website builder—no system for payments, no connectivity to booking platforms such as HomeAway and Booking.com; it really was a light website builder. It was simple, and it was effective in getting people to sign up.

Phil and Jon Fabio used their weekends to work on the MVP while keeping their day jobs. Still, the MVP didn't take long to come out. While it wasn't effective as a true home base for vacation-rental owners, it could still be considered a major success because it showed off the future vision to customers. The MVP was also effective in making vacation-rental owners and managers care about the product, even if it wasn't very good yet. After all, they cared enough to complain about the product's inadequacies and they gave many suggestions of what they wished it could do. The fact that they cared enough to make suggestions about what could make Futurestay better, Phil observed, meant there was a tremendous opportunity afoot. The MVP got the audience interested in what Futurestay could become, and it did so without breaking the bank.

IN HINDSIGHT, WE SHOULD HAVE ROLLED OUT ONE SIMPLE APP FOR SUBTLE AT THE START AND THEN COMMUNICATED OUR VISION

Unlike Futurestay, we never *once* took user feedback into consideration as a way that we could expand our product. Not only would we have gotten Subtle out there with one-eighth of the effort, but we would have gotten to know our potential audience as well. Instead, we spent all of our time in the cave, building and rebuilding. We could have marketed our idea with an MVP, found an audience, learned more about their interests, and generated some real revenue to put back into Subtle's development, all with very few resources needed. Had we gone that route, my money could have been stretched out for so much longer.

I had a team that was inexperienced at the time with making apps from start to finish, so we just kept going in circles with no direction and too much to do. I was also very inexperienced with managing a team on such a project, which was the even bigger problem. I was too focused on my team's failures while neglecting my own. I should have seen that there was no cohesion, but I didn't have the leadership or the know-how yet to do that.

1. I learned that you should never take the concept of the team for granted. You shouldn't expect them to succeed if you can't offer them any kind of direction. Successes are always the result of team efforts, but failure usually stems from the top. It is critical, as a leader, to identify what could have caused the failure, why it wasn't recognized prior, and how to resolve it moving forward.

2. I should never have put all my eggs in one basket. Investing every dollar I had into Subtle was foolish. I wasn't looking out for everyone's best interests in the long term; instead, I was blinded by short-term greed. I learned that if you're going to burn the boats to take over an island, you should at least be prepared for the fact that if you don't get the island, there won't be any options left.

Back then, I wouldn't have looked back and listed everything that went wrong with Subtle and what I should have done differently. This would only happen once I started to figure out self-awareness.

Being self-aware is not only about identifying *why* you feel and do the things that you do; it's also recognizing *what* causes you to feel those ways and do those things. How do you handle it when someone on your team fails to perform and hides it from you? How do you handle it when a customer is upset? How do you maintain peace and understanding when you have third-party vendors in control of something that you depend on to succeed? I'm not just talking about this from a business operational sense (although that is important) but from a personal behavioral sense, too.

SELF-AWARENESS BEGINS BY ASKING WHAT, NOT WHY

Tasha Eurich, the author of the book *Insight*, explains why those who are most self-aware use the context of what versus why. It is because why doesn't help us. If I said to you, "Why aren't you feeling good about your business?" you would probably answer something such as "Not enough revenue" or "I'm unhappy and stressed." However, if I ask you *what* is making you not feel good about your business, there's a greater potential that you'll come up with more substantial answers. Instead of just describing your feelings, you'll list concrete problems that can possibly be solved.

Tasha doesn't outright dismiss the importance of noting the whys. Those are still a critical piece of the self-awareness equation. So let me introduce you to the three-whys equation. The concept is simple: you ask "why" to each "what" explanation you give yourself, and it takes you down to the real root of a problem, question, or feeling that you have.

Let's say you have an employee who is looking to quit. They say they do not like their job, that this isn't the right fit for them. Ask them why they think so. Their response might be that the atmosphere and culture have changed—they used to enjoy showing up to the office, but now it feels toxic and they would rather avoid it at all costs. Again, you ask why they think the culture has changed. After thinking it over, they might explain that one of the new team members is always too cynical and impacts the entire team dynamic and morale. This is the power of the three-whys equation—it leads you to the what. And by asking what, you not only know the result that needs to be changed but also what can be done to change it.

One of the most helpful tools of self-awareness is keeping a journal. I always have one on me (physical or digital) and write down everything, from daily accomplishments to how I am feeling in the moment. I use these notes to identify trends in myself, which in turn helps remind myself to stay cool, calm, and collected when the going gets tough. The journal lets me see how things play out long term with my emotions. I have all of this documentation on myself and my processes that I can always refer back to. As an added plus, writing in a journal always gives my brain some rest from the digital world.

BE TOUGH AND COMPETENT

Eugene (Gene) F. Kranz, former flight director for NASA during its Gemini and Apollo programs, has a saying that he made sure everyone in his flight control would understand: *be tough and competent*. I like this because it eliminates the other made-up pressures that people tend to put on themselves. Instead, it encourages the mindset of always remaining resilient in times of stress, pressure, and uncertainty. It also discourages from overthinking too much.

This is the same mindset I apply to journaling. I always strive to identify where I am not up to par with how I need to conduct myself as an entrepreneur, a CEO, a service provider to my clients, a mentor, and a role model. I also constantly try to identify areas where I am not giving myself enough credit. I need to know where to put my time, energy, and soul into improving. Above all, I need to understand how the things I do each day align with what my heart tells me I most enjoy.

Most of us have been raised to "suck it up" when feeling upset, angered, flustered, frustrated, or confused. But emotions are a natural part of ourselves to be embraced and understood. The idea that we need to bottle it up is not only a terrible mindset to have, but it also leads to unsustainable entrepreneurship. Emotions stem from real, underlying issues; we need to identify these issues in order to become better leaders for our companies, team members, customers, clients, you name it.

Being open about how you're feeling matters. If you receive an email that frustrates you, identify what frustrates you about it, and then ask yourself the three whys. There is no point in being passive-aggressive or just ignoring it and letting it simmer in your head. I am not suggesting you go and have a volcanic eruption as I did with Subtle, but it is much healthier to be honest (in a mature way) about what you think in the moment and turn it into a learning experience for yourself and the people whom you're working with.

Your exercise:

What is troubling you right now? What do you feel positive about? It can be anything from your business to something else that is on your mind a lot. Write down the whats, and really challenge yourself with the whys.

What? _____

Why? _____

Why? _____

Why? _____

What? _____

Why? _____

Why? _____

Why? _____

CREATE A MORNING RITUAL FOR YOURSELF

I have programmed myself to have better mornings, which really do set the tone of the day. No matter if I am at home, staying in a hotel, or even at my father's house, I make sure that my ideal morning ritual gets done. Immediately upon waking, before my brain begins racing with the day's activities and before I dwell on the mountain of to-dos ahead, I immediately jump into the shower. I refuse to look at my phone because the notifications are going to suck me in and then I'll blow the most valuable hour of the day. Getting into the shower is an easy way I can enforce that policy. This is *my* time, and being in the shower is perhaps one of the only times in a day when I am truly alone. No emails, no phone calls, no text messages, no notifications, no distractions, no other people. Just me and my thoughts.

As the warm water hits me, I adjust from sleeping to wakefulness. My thoughts aren't swirling anymore, and I can be focused or even give my brain a break and not think at all. It's my form of meditation. I can slowly begin to focus on everything I am grateful for. I think about my fondest memories—the times as a kid that I used to go to Six Flags on the weekends, hanging out on the boardwalk, the early days of Chop Dawg, the day I first brought my first dog home, spending time with my family, and all the things that make me warm inside and remind me why life is worth living.

I also focus on what I have an abundance of—my home, my relationships, my business, and the opportunities I'm lucky to have. Finally, I focus on my why: what motivates me, pushes me, makes me excel, challenges me to become better at what I love to do. I use the context of my gratitude, life, and my fortunes to remind myself how good I have it, and how my push and quest to continue to build, create, and help comes from this. This is what makes me want to become the best I can be.

Before I can truly begin my day, I go work out at the gym. I strategically purchased a home within a five-minute walk of a gym so that I never have an excuse to miss a day. This is where I need to pay my dues, to keep my body strong as well as my mind. I lift weights, run on the treadmill, stretch. With my blood flowing, my muscles moving, I'm finally ready to take on anything the day has in store for me. My mind has been prepared and my body has been pushed. Now it is time to work on my business.

I know how quickly I can enter a depressive state when I let my emotions override my logic and let my fears and greed take over. The reality is, there are days when I still get short-tempered. There are still times I receive emails that make me angry. There are days where I am easily annoyed. There are moments when I want to be doing anything else. But by being able to catch myself as these emotions happen and being mentally prepared for such events to occur, I can walk away from these moments of irrationality before I do anything stupid. When I'm feeling rational again, I'll come back to it. I recognize the whys that are causing them. Slowly but surely, I have become better at catching myself in these moments of "quick emotion."

I am human, and so are you. Be open about your thoughts and feelings to others, and you will have a fighting chance to overcome the ways that you self-sabotage yourself every day.

ONE OF THE THINGS I'VE BECOME OBSESSED WITH IS HOW TO MAKE THE MOST OF THE TIME I HAVE

One thing you'll see me harp on is how I don't think enough people value their time. OK, so what am I most efficient at? What drains my energy? What are the things that take me a long time to complete? What makes me feel like I've wasted my time versus spending it well? These are the questions I ask myself as I go through my daily routines running Chop Dawg. I want to understand where my value as an entrepreneur, a leader, a CEO, a colleague, a team member, a marketer, and a business-development persona can best be served.

I would have quickly hit my ceiling if I hadn't hired people to cover the work coming in after I had been on the news as a kid, but some entrepreneurs can (and sometimes have to) go a really long time without hiring a single person. One such person that I know is John Accardi, who currently owns Accardi Products.

Accardi Products produces and sells care packages under the brands CollegeBox, CraveBox, and Canopy Snacks. While Accardi Products now has a bigger team and a 13,000-square-foot warehouse facility, it took a long time to get to that point. John spent four years doing everything himself—he spent ten hours per day making care packages and then would work on marketing before going to bed. For a long time, he didn't need employees because there wasn't enough work to be done. But even when he was making a lot of sales, he didn't hire right away. He eventually realized that doing everything himself meant he had a ceiling for the demand he could hit because he never had time to grow the business. By not hiring someone new when he needed to, he was sabotaging himself.

So John made an investment and rented a small warehouse space and hired someone to make the care packages so that he could focus on growing Accardi Products. That incremental move allowed him to get a second employee just six months later. He recently hired his third, fourth, fifth, sixth, and seventh employees. With a full team now, he has positioned himself to spend all of his time working *on* his business rather than *in* his business.

Just like John, I felt the need to do everything in the beginning before it felt justified to hire someone. Over the years, I've realized I am not good at everything and never will be. I've learned that by sticking to the best use of my own time and delegating everything else, I can build a better operational structure for my company.

When talking to John, he was sure to emphasize to me, "Only hire when there is plenty of work to be done." And I agree. If I had not operated this way myself, I would have been hemorrhaging money. Instead, whenever I made a hire, it was always because there was something that needed to be done that I couldn't do or could not do as well. Every person on my team is better at doing at least one thing than I am at doing it. And there is always work to get done.

I love the social aspects of business development and being a CEO. I love that through networking, connecting, and meeting with others, I have been able to improve my conversation and listening skills. I love being able to apply a mixture of salesmanship, critical thinking, long-term strategic planning, and pure friendship, all mixed into one bag that allows me to help potential clients, new clients, and existing clients. It is also what allows me to give value to my team when working with them on what is happening operationally at Chop Dawg.

I not only know I thrive on social interaction, but the extrovert in me also allows me to identify and work on opportunities at scale. I've come to learn that a one-hour meeting with the right person can accomplish a lot. During that one hour, I help a business owner translate their idea into a realistic vision that could create jobs. I can give someone the confidence in their vision that they didn't quite have before. I can help them articulate their vision in plain English. Over time, that one meeting could be the catalyst that turns one idea into hundreds of thousands of dollars and millions of users and impacts thousands of lives in a positive manner. All from that original one-hour meeting. That excites the hell out of me.

On the opposite end of the spectrum, while I'm fascinated by programming and design (and an enthusiast of this on the side), I really don't enjoy *working on* either trade. Honestly, for me to work as a developer or designer would be company sabotage at this point. For me, it's tedious work that drains me emotionally and mentally. But for the designers and developers on my team, it's the complete opposite.

There are countless entrepreneurs who will read this, who hate the extroverted aspects that I love, and instead prefer the introverted roles necessary for an operation to succeed. That is OK, as long as you have someone who can fill the roles you hate!

THERE IS A REASON WHY WE BEGIN THE FRAMEWORK WITH SELF-AWARENESS. WITHOUT IT, YOU'RE NOT CAPABLE OF LEARNING OR LEVERAGING ANY OF THE OTHER PRINCIPLES THIS BOOK WILL PROVIDE

As you read the remaining chapters, I will challenge you to question yourself, your beliefs, and your capabilities. You need to consider yourself the same way scientists and researchers consider data. We work with the best information that we know but never accept what we know as the guaranteed answer. Success requires having the hunger to learn, practice continually, challenge your routines, improve, reiterate, and yes, question yourself.

As you complete each chapter, think about how you're performing in each principle listed in the framework and articulate it with a score of 0 to 100 percent: *self-awareness, empathy, leadership, short-term thinking, long-term thinking, economics, operations,* and *purpose.*

The lower the score percentage, the more improvement you will need to become a well-rounded entrepreneur. The closer to 100 percent, the stronger you are at each individual principle. The closer you get, the more efficient and fulfilled you'll be. You're not necessarily meant to hit a flawless 100 percent across the board (candidly, I do not think this is even possible), but this is the constant goal that you should forever be trying to reach.

Here is an example of the framework filled out following the methodology described above and throughout this book:

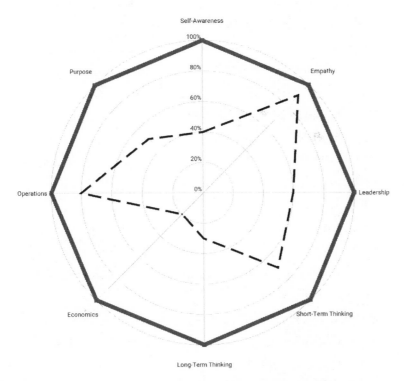

In this example, here is where this one individual has ranked himself or herself:

- Self-awareness: 40 percent
- Empathy: 90 percent
- Leadership: 60 percent
- Short-term thinking: 70 percent
- Long-term thinking: 30 percent
- Economics: 20 percent
- Operations: 80 percent
- Purpose: 50 percent

There is nothing to be ashamed of if you're at 40 percent and nothing to gloat about if you're at 90 percent. You're a work of art, a master of your craft, and striving to become better for yourself and others. Most do not take the time even to assign a numerical value to keep track of, but you're not like most people, are you? The only thing you could ever be ashamed of is lying to yourself. Assigning yourself a number that isn't true is just self-sabotage.

This is why self-awareness is so critical. Without it, you can't understand context or become grateful for what you have or what you will have. Self-awareness ties everything together and is the universal principle that will apply to everything else. Self-awareness is about being open to yourself, challenging yourself, understanding yourself, and holding yourself accountable. No one else is looking, so it's all up to you.

Learning self-awareness is the only way that I was able to turn around Chop Dawg after my failure with Subtle. I also would not have been able to write this book if it wasn't for self-awareness. When Subtle failed, I wanted to blame everyone for our shortcomings. I blamed my team for not producing. It took a few years and a lot of practice with self-awareness, but it is clear as day to me now that it was never their fault. I wasn't open about my thoughts and I wasn't aware of our shortcomings. I didn't even understand my own feelings at the time, let alone the ability to articulate them. I didn't have the wherewithal to speak up when things were starting to go downhill, nor the maturity to sit down with my team and talk out our problems.

Chop Dawg is only successful today because I don't just practice self-awareness personally; it's a maxim that has spread across the team. Even our clients have become more self-aware through our being a positive influence. To me, it is the very top purpose of the Entrepreneur's Framework: self-awareness is the guiding star that will allow you to become successful with every other principle of the framework.

CHAPTER 5

EMPATHY

After I dropped out of college in 2012 (the year before Subtle), I felt like I had all the time in the world. I no longer had school to hold me back from committing to my company full-time. And for the first time in my life, I had a small team working beside me. Things felt like they were really coming along! I had a real business, and we were all hungry. The team and I all felt like we had a chip on our shoulders, ready to prove to the world that we didn't need to get "real jobs." By this point, we were swimming in client work, all thanks to word of mouth, organic SEO, and media coverage.

We were at an awkward phase as far as operations go, with growing pains similar to those of a teenager. I mean, we were still a team of teens ourselves: our voices always cracked; our skin was covered in pimples and blemishes. Although we had plenty of work coming in, we were starting to face some new harsh realities. For one thing, I no longer had the "teenage entrepreneur" story that felt unique to me—more and more teens were appearing on the news talking about their startups. *The Social Network* had come out in theaters, and young college dropout entrepreneurs had become more mainstream. Our market was growing, and firms that were doing exactly what we were doing were sprouting up like toadstools. These firms that were sprouting up seemed more sophisticated; our operation looked two-bit in comparison. Now we had to convince new prospects to take us seriously. With saturation and mass acceptance comes commoditization. By commoditization, I mean the service we provided didn't seem different enough anymore, and our image was becoming a liability. We didn't offer anything unique over the more experienced firms. So what could we do differently?

The other issue coming up was that even though many businesses were finally understanding they must be online, I could tell from a lot of websites that it was more of a begrudging acceptance. When having a website became the new standard, there was this flood of begrudging customers who had previously rejected the idea. A lot of companies just wanted the lowest price possible for the most minimal product. They treated building websites as if they were copy-and-pasting their Yellow Pages entry online.

It was our goal to find customers who weren't begrudgingly going online, but we were also looking for the customers who still weren't fully convinced. Why? Because maybe if they moved their presence online through our influence, we could make sure that their websites had a much higher standard of quality. This would make us look better than anyone else, and then we could finally have higher-priced clients. Easy, right? This was our chance to prove ourselves.

AFTER SEVERAL HOURS OF DELIBERATIONS ABOUT HOW WE WOULD REACH PEOPLE, WE ARRIVED AT A MARKETING IDEA THAT *FELT* INCREDIBLE TO US

It was a simple idea in theory. Why not just directly write to small business owners exactly where they live? We all thought sending a direct mail campaign would work beautifully. Now, I know you are probably already moaning at the idea of a mailer. But there was a time when mailers were the king of direct marketing. Because we could make the direct appeal to handpicked addresses, to us, it seemed like direct mail would make for that physical connection. If we got people to stop, open, and read what we had to say, they couldn't possibly refuse, right? We also knew most of the small business owners we would be targeting with a mailer campaign would probably be older people. It made perfect sense to us that because they knew they needed to have an online presence but didn't jump in, direct mail would be the place.

But we needed to figure out how we could be distinctive. I was watching *Back to the Future Part II* with Eddie when the idea sprang into my head. At the end of the movie, Doc Brown, the crazy white-haired scientist who invented the time-traveling DeLorean, is accidentally sent back in time to the nineteenth century, leaving the main character, Marty McFly, stuck in 1955. As soon as Marty McFly realizes that he is stuck in the past, a man from the US delivery service informs him that the postal service received instructions from nearly a century ago to provide a signed letter to him at this time, at this place. Marty immediately realizes that this is from Doc. The letter, as Marty reads it, looks as old as it is, nearly falling apart in his hands, belonging to a time that has long ago passed.

Just like that—inspiration for our mailer!

The mailer would need to hit home for our audience, to evoke the fear that if they didn't get on the bandwagon, they were going to be *left behind*. So we would make a mailer that looked antiquated: everything from the envelope, to the stamp, to the wax seal on the back. The letter would be presented as if it belonged to the late 1800s.

WE FELT LIKE EVERYTHING ABOUT OUR MAILER CAMPAIGN WAS WELL THOUGHT-OUT AND CAREFULLY PUT TOGETHER

We researched every registered small business in the state

of New Jersey that didn't already have a website. Once we discovered the owners, we found their *home addresses*. We felt so crafty. Our competitors would probably just take the "easy" way of sending directly to the business. But we didn't want to risk some employee reading it and merely throwing it out.

We quickly discovered that we couldn't just buy envelopes that looked like they had been ravaged by time. So we turned it into an arts and crafts project. We soaked white envelopes in upside down garbage can lids that were filled with water and tea bags. The tea bags dyed the envelopes brown; after drying, each one would feel as if it was going to fall apart. (To ensure that they wouldn't fall apart, we single-handedly blow-dried each one after soaking.) We had to wait about a week after the tea bag-soaked envelopes were thoroughly dry before handwriting (in fountain pen, no less) the names and address on these envelopes. We had no room for error—if we wrote a mistake or there was something that was hard to read on the envelope, it would be lost in the mail forever. We ordered custom old-fashioned stamps from the US Postal Service, and finally, to give our letters as much authenticity as possible, we stamped a wax seal with the Chop Dawg logo on the back. This letter really looked as though it had been sent one century ago.

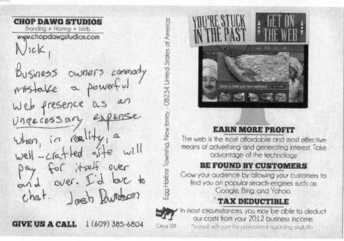

But with our first order, we made a few errors. For one thing, the wax stamps were way too large, and would not fit in US Postal Service sorting machines. I also should have known that my handwriting was horrible and looked like a fourth grader's. I remember dropping the letters off at the post office in three giant brown grocery bags and seeing the clerk look at me with disdain. Still, we assured ourselves that every single letter would be opened and that none of our time or dollars would go to waste. It didn't matter that the costs were adding up for this mailer; I *knew* it was going to work.

The following Monday, Eddie and I glued ourselves next to the phone in a conference room at Richard Stockton University, ready to answer the barrage of expected calls. We couldn't contain our excitement; whatever work we had to do, we just couldn't focus on it. We couldn't stop fantasizing about how this was going to bring us to the big time and turn Chop Dawg into a sales machine. *We could replicate this mailer campaign around the country,* we dreamed.

AN HOUR WENT BY, THEN TWO HOURS, THEN SEVERAL HOURS. THE ENTIRE DAY WENT BY, AND NOTHING HAPPENED

Not a phone call, not an email. One day turned into a few days, and before we knew it, it was a few weeks later with zero responses. Our joyous excitement and enthusiasm for the future turned into bleak despair. Eddie and I couldn't believe it. I had a theory that perhaps the mailer service didn't send out our letters because they didn't look right. Or perhaps they fell apart in their sorting facilities because of what we did with the dye ink. But when we started getting occasional letters bounced back to my home address, we knew the mailers had been sent. We began to have doubts.

Maybe we made a mistake on the mailer—did we have the wrong telephone number listed? No, it was right. Maybe the wrong website link? Nope, that was right, too.

One day, the phone did ring. I couldn't contain my excitement and handed the phone to Eddie to answer. He put the call on speaker. The caller explained how he never opens mail that he doesn't recognize, but he was so captivated by our letter and the fact that we found his home address that he had to open ours. OK, we were excited now. He applauded us for not only designing something so original but also for how great of a message it was. Finally, Eddie got down to the brass tacks. *How can we help him with his website?* Right then and there, he stopped Eddie.

"Oh, no, no, no. I am so sorry for causing any confusion. I don't need a new website. The page we have is more than fine. Most of our customers have been coming to us for years. We only put up a website because it was free from this so-and-so service. I just wanted to call and let you guys know how much I loved your letter and to continue doing what you are doing!"

And click. He hung up. That was it. Eddie stared at me. I stared at the table. We both couldn't believe it. We discovered the truth about why no one was calling. Despite all the effort we'd put into the presentation of the mailer, we were selling to people who just didn't want to be sold to.

Too often, I see people try to jump right in and force the sale. But how well can I sell you on something if I don't know about *you* and your current needs? Too many people fail to sell by being too laser-focused on getting to the transaction itself and ignoring the human conversation that really leads to the sale. I would say that true sales isn't "selling" at all. Now I really think of it as a mission of fact-finding, educating, and helping people to find a solution to their needs. Find out the needs, then serve the needs. Be a detective, not a salesperson. And to be a great detective, you need to establish trust with everyone you speak to.

WITH OUR MAILER, WE HAD BEEN WAY TOO FOCUSED ON ONE ASSUMPTION

"Being stuck in the past." We genuinely thought that this one fear would drive everyone in droves to seek our service. But by focusing on this one assumption, we missed everything else. What we didn't realize at the time was that one sentence on a mailer with high production value wasn't going to establish trust. "Being stuck in the past" could have been something that our mailer recipients feared, but then why would they want to go with us? Why should they even trust us, especially with that fourth-grader handwriting? And we weren't educating our would-be customers at all. Why would having a website prevent business owners from feeling left behind? We were really just throwing a slogan at someone. We never educated business owners on how they could make more money by having a website. We were talking to an audience that purposely didn't have a website already, because they did not understand the value of having one!

Despite handpicking all of the addresses we sent the mailer to, we hadn't learned much of anything about our recipients besides that they were small business owners. We assumed everyone would feel the urgent need to prepare for the future and would recognize the common sense that, to us, felt universal. It never occurred to us that maybe they didn't *want* a website.

Connecting people with their needs is something that empathetic entrepreneurs do very well. It comes through *understanding* other people's experiences, even those far removed from your own. While you can't possibly feel the *direct* pain and joy that others go through, you'll start to understand how a diverse group of people think. I cannot emphasize enough how helpful a skill empathy is.

Jennifer Pahlka is the founder and executive director of Code for America, a network of people using technology to make government services simpler, more effective, and easier to use. The only way that Code for America is effective is if there is empathy behind the technology. She is very aware of this with every project the developers work on. How can you fix something if you don't know how bad it is yourself? When the developers at Code for America were creating an app to address California's issues with their food stamp program (CalFresh), they couldn't just build something from scratch first. So Jennifer had her programmers enroll in current government programs so they could feel the problems themselves before trying to fix them. One issue in particular they hoped to solve was why so many recipients failed to renew their claims and kept dropping off. By becoming food stamp recipients themselves, the programmers experienced the full frustrations of the system. After experiencing how time-intensive and nonintuitive CalFresh was, the programmers were able to build an app that truly addressed the problems people faced when enrolling in the program.

Of course, to understand and feel for the lives of *all* people is a gargantuan task. That's why entrepreneurs should pick a slice of humanity to truly understand. To understand your customer, you have to understand that needs come in multiple layers.

Your exercise:

The first step is to identify the broader differences between needs and wants.

Knowing how to tell a need from a want will change a lot about what you'll offer to your customer. You can see sometimes that your wants and your needs conflict with each other. The more specific your wants and needs are, the less likely they are to match with someone else's.

I was recently thinking about something that I want, which is to add a recording studio to my home office so that I can film videos and record podcasts for Chop Dawg. I could potentially rationalize this as a need, but it's really more of a want.

WHAT DO I WANT?	WHAT DO I NEED TO GET THIS DONE?	IS THERE ANYTHING ELSE THAT I NEED MORE?	DO I NEED THIS TO STAY IN BUSINESS?
A home-office recording studio	Money and time	Yes	No

My real need is to keep my business running for as long as possible. My business can survive without the home-office recording studio, and there are more direct ways that I can bring in recurring revenue.

But the fact that I arrived at even *wanting* a recording studio for my business tells me that I'm in a much different position than someone who is trying to just keep the lights on. When I was in that position, I didn't even think about wanting a recording studio. But now, I'm in the comfortable position of wanting the luxuries that can boost my business. Being able to distinguish between wants and needs is a part of being empathetic.

So now go through this exercise of distinguishing your own wants and needs.

Step 1: What is your life like? What are the things you take for granted?

Step 2: Now imagine that one of these things was taken away from you. Your computer, electricity, your shoes. What might life be like for you then?

Step 3: Now think about someone you know. How is their life different from yours? How does that affect their individual needs?

Step 4: Put yourself in the shoes of a stranger located somewhere else. How does their location make life different from yours? Does it affect their needs relative to yours?

DON'T FORGET, THESE EXERCISE STEPS ARE MOOT WITHOUT BEING ABLE TO LISTEN TO OTHERS

Empathy is the understanding, appreciation, and ability to step into someone's life and feel how they live. You can't get to that point without being able to *listen*. Believe me, I don't claim to be a great listener yet. I'm getting there, but it is hard sometimes when my own mind is swirling with ideas, counterpoints, and to-dos. Being able to truly listen to people and make them feel listened to is something that has taken me years to be good at.

Jeff Booth is the cofounder of BuildDirect, an online marketplace for heavyweight home improvement products. He considers empathy and listening as a true business skill. After nearly collapsing during the 2008 financial crisis, BuildDirect turned things around by quickly adapting. Last year, they opened a global supply-chain platform for heavyweight appliances and goods.

Before starting BuildDirect with his cofounder, Rob Banks, Jeff was a home builder. When he was on the job, he experienced many of the frustrations of his clients firsthand. One thing that he found that was completely missing in the construction industry was an online marketplace where you could order construction materials easily. This made him question why something like this didn't exist.

I've seen many entrepreneurs who are looking to quickly fix existing problems while not getting down to the root cause. They aren't experiencing their own frustrations firsthand that can then be turned into a business. According to Jeff, "Real empathy requires going beyond the Band-Aid solution and investing in an actual cure." This isn't the easy path, of course, because identifying the deep root cause requires empathy as a hard skill. It comes through truly understanding and then solving someone else's pains and frustrations. This principle doesn't just extend to the customers but also to everyone in your business's orbit.

Jeff has used this maxim as the foundation for building his business. It's also allowed him to adapt and find new opportunities. Rather than only moving forward with what brings revenue in the short term, Jeff always listens to customer attitudes. Without listening to these attitudes, you end up missing out on the silent shifts that occur without your knowing it.

I'VE HAD TO DEAL WITH FALLING INTO THE CALL-RESPONSE TRAP WHEN LISTENING

It used to be that I would listen, but simultaneously I was formulating my response in my head while still "listening." This would make it difficult for me to truly listen, and I'd usually come up with a response that didn't really fit the conversation. Too many times, I've shifted the conversation entirely to myself, and then the person I was talking to felt the need to do the same.

I was getting a bad feeling that I was not as great on the phone as I thought I was. So I decided to start recording my meetings. When listening to the recordings, I found that there were a lot of negative qualities about myself that I had been oblivious to.

I found that I was:

1. **Interruptive**. I would seek opportunities to jump in with my counterpoint before the other person was finished.
2. **Dominant in the conversation**. I love to explain things and talk, but I was sucking all of the air out of the conversation, turning my conversation partner into just a recipient. (I used to keep track of this manually with a stopwatch. In person this is harder to tell, but that's why it's good to associate yourself with people who aren't afraid to give you critical feedback.) Even if you're interesting, people get sick of being lectured. Good conversation is a balanced dance of listening and talking.
3. **Too much of a debater**. This was especially a problem of mine when I was first working with clients. I had preconceived notions of what was right, and so I would shut myself off to new opinions or alternative viewpoints. I would try to "win" arguments.

I cannot emphasize enough how gaining empathy requires a wealth of information gathering. By keeping the conversation between the two of you, you can extract a lot more information. There's a unique challenge in the New Economy that has sprouted up because of the wealth of information at our disposal. People feel well-informed by reading lots of articles about problems that others are going through but mistake that knowledge for having empathy. I don't think that direct conversation can ever be substituted as the best exchange of information, though.

I've found over the years that I've gotten the most out of conversations when I purely listen to the other person without *thinking* of a response while they're talking. Once I've collected this information, I can come up with a response after a quick, deliberate pause when it's my turn. I used to think that I couldn't come up with responses like this on the fly, because I didn't want to pause to think about what I was saying. But you'd be surprised how easy that is to do when you listen and observe, rather than just thinking about what you are going to say next. It's really all about being a detective. You end up walking away from conversations with so much more information that you can work with.

HOW WE CONFUSED OUR SYMPATHY FOR EMPATHY

In retrospect, we couldn't possibly have been empathetic to the small businesses we sent the mailer to. We hadn't connected with any of these owners before, so we really didn't understand their perspective at all. We assumed that they wanted to move into the New Economy, but we didn't understand why these people didn't *want* to be a part of the New Economy—we had never owned a pre-internet business like they did. We were just shoving our perspective down their throats.

We had felt "sympathy" for these people because we saw, from our vantage point, that they were being left behind. They were inferior to us. But on the contrary, a lot of these people didn't feel like they were being left behind at all. Because we didn't understand the position of business owners who didn't want to make the transition and didn't feel the need to (who doesn't think they need a website?), we couldn't educate or build trust. We just didn't respect their reasons for not wanting an online presence in the first place.

EMPATHETIC INDIVIDUALS UNDERSTAND IF YOU DO SOMETHING WITH INTEGRITY THAT OFFERS REAL VALUE AND UTILITY, IT WILL REALLY RESONATE WITH PEOPLE

Let's go back to PiperWai, the natural deodorant company founded by Sarah Ribner and Jess Edelstein. Jess originally came up with the idea for the formula and made it herself based on her own pain. She found it next to impossible to find a deodorant that wasn't full of chemicals but actually worked. The natural deodorants that were on the market either made customers smell even worse or just plain didn't do anything. What resonated with me most of all when hanging out with both Jess and Sarah was how much they emphasized that they would never *ever* sell a product that they wouldn't use themselves.

This is a lesson that I needed to learn in 2012, and I've

worked on building it into my DNA for the last seven years. Today, I strive to solve problems that people *really* have, rather than just ones that I've come up with.

Your exercise:

Think about whether you've ever tried to solve a problem for someone, without asking first if they wanted to be helped. A common trap that I still fall into is becoming too excited about solving a problem, as opposed to helping someone out. All too often, I'm quick to jump to solutions before the other person is ready to get to that stage. Have you done this? If so, what do you think keeps making you do it? If not, how do you avoid it?

_____

_____

You can't find your purpose without understanding others first. Empathy can turn a passion into a purpose. It is what allows you to discover what it is that fulfills you, drives you, and moves you to impact others and create value for others at scale.

CHAPTER 6

LEADERSHIP

It was early 2012, and I had stumbled upon something extraordinary. I didn't fully comprehend it at the time, but I had accidentally discovered a tool that would allow me to turn Chop Dawg from a company with virtually no app sales to one generating millions in revenue. I discovered the power of e-commerce through Twitter.

An individual tweeted out to the world that he needed an app developer to build his dream app. Coincidentally, this was at the same time that we'd decided that Chop Dawg was to become an app development agency. We were no longer a website-design-only firm and we were hungry. We were also borderline desperate for any work we could get our hands on.

E-commerce may sound commonplace on social media today. But back in 2012, this wasn't the norm. Not yet. This is before Twitter became overrun with bots, scheduled posts, clichéd social media influencers, and everyday folks trying to upsell you. This was back when Twitter was in its prime, with its pre-algorithm-driven feeds.

The pre-algorithm-driven Twitter feed provided real-time tweets from the people you followed and genuinely cared to read about. The feed was something that could be spontaneous and exciting, and had it not been for the real-time feed, I may have never found the tweet at all. With the real-time feed, I was one of the first to read that tweet and had the chance to take an at bat before anyone else could. I was dead set on hitting a home run, no matter the costs.

With a mixture of unvalidated confidence and immature optimism, I took advantage of what at the time felt like divine intervention. I explained to this individual that we would be, in essence, their saviors. I assured him that we had the knowledge, the know-how, the team, and the *experience* to help.

But as you already know by now, that wasn't exactly the truth. Don't get me wrong, we *believed* in all of this. We felt it in our bones. We had the passion, that internal fire, and yes, we did have the knowledge, know-how, and the team. But the experience part? The part where we would have to deliver on our big promises? That was pushing it.

Chop Dawg had existed for almost four years, but we weren't 225-plus apps deep with experience as we are today. No, we had made a grand total of *one*. That was PartyHopp, the app that had fueled my passion for getting into building apps in the first place. That *was* experience, so, again, not a lie but not entirely the full truth either. It felt, in many ways, how most pizza shops would call themselves the "world's best pizza"—they might be, but who is to judge or say?

I had all of the fire and passion of a leader back in 2012, but I genuinely believed that overselling ourselves was the only way we could get the client we wanted. We needed to get that at bat we were desperate for, at any cost.

But I really *did believe* we could do it, and we really needed the work.

WITHIN A WEEK OF THAT TWEET, MY HEAD OF PROGRAMMING AT THE TIME, BRANDON TELLER, AND I WERE ON AN AMTRAK BOUND FOR NEW YORK CITY

We were set to meet the lead for lunch, and I remember telling Brandon that we weren't going to blow this. The meeting went as well as I could have ever hoped for. Even when they asked us to walk them through some of our prior experiences, Brandon and I were on our A game. We only had PartyHopp to talk about, and fortunately, that was all we needed for this meeting. We walked them through the whole process of how we made PartyHopp into a revenue-generating app. That was all the proof they needed; they didn't ask us about any other clients. Within a few short weeks after our meeting, the contracts were signed, the down payment was made, and my team was off to the races. This was our shot to hit something out of the park.

But when actually delivering on our promises, the problems came about almost right away. Unlike today, we were doing everything that had to get done at once. There was no defined methodology, reasoning, or organization. Today, we always focus on design first, before writing a single line of code at Chop Dawg. We eliminate the possibility of misinterpretation and miscommunication from biting us in the butt, causing delays and hiccups in any app project. Back then, we didn't organize ourselves at all. We just didn't have the experience or the expertise to realize such problems could and would exist. That opened the opportunity for endless bugs and revisions in programming, and nightmarish scenarios in design.

In hindsight, this resulted in some unforeseen (but preventable) issues, as new designs were in direct conflict with bits of code already in place and completed prior. Because we had never bothered to write a proper project plan, it felt like we were working on a moving target while also blindfolded and intoxicated. The team put in five times the work they needed to.

Naively, I assumed if the client didn't see every facet of their project happening at once, they would be dissatisfied, even if the work was being done to get their apps completed. But of course, I was wrong there. Because we were spreading ourselves thin, we were getting constant client feedback on designs, and in result, the code was breaking with the constant changes we were making. We promised a timetable of milestones to the client, but we failed to meet each one. We kept telling the client that if they just stopped always wanting to change things, we could get the job done. The client would always snipe back that if we could just get the job done right, they wouldn't have to. This stressed us out, and we felt like hamsters on a spinning wheel. The outcome was disastrous. We constantly were bickering with the client. That should never happen.

Three months after we had expected to have the job completed, we were still working overtime on a half-functioning product when the client said they'd finally had it.

They fired us.

A swing and a miss. We struck out at what felt like our first and only at bat in the major league. How did this happen?

1. I had overpromised, and then we underdelivered. This was not out of laziness, but because I had overestimated the capability of my team. We were working hard, but I could never communicate to the team exactly what the client wanted. We didn't even have our client aligned with what they wanted. I should have been able to get everyone on the same page, but I didn't have the project management skills yet.

2. I had not anticipated that just because we were able to do one project successfully, that didn't mean we were qualified to do another. With small business websites, we had been working on a service that could be easily replicated. I naively thought that apps would be easily replicated across projects, too.

3. Even when things weren't going right, I didn't have the courage to be transparent with the client. I thought I could hide behind the curtain of attentive service, but attentive service is moot without the deliverables to back it up. In the end, all the positive meetings in the world couldn't mask the fact that we made a broken product.

Years later, I am thankful that we were fired.

I am not remotely OK with the fact that we did let down

these two individuals—that is forever on my conscience. But this setback (along with Subtle) forced me to look at exactly what caused us to fail and learn how to ensure that this would never happen again. Otherwise, we would be doomed to repeat the same mistakes.

I INCORRECTLY THOUGHT AT THE TIME THAT LEADERSHIP COULD ONLY COME FROM SOLELY ONE INDIVIDUAL

Leadership is a shared mindset. Individual leaders can be catalysts for change, but without a collective effort, nothing can get done. A collective is always more powerful than an individual.

I had programmed myself to think that leaders are solely responsibility for everything. The early successes of Chop Dawg, before I even had a team, made me think that the whole operation would fail without me. It felt good to think that the only way my company could stay in business was if I were around all the time. I swore *I* was *the* visionary, the only person who could do it all. I loved the idea of being that guy who could heroically swoop in and make all of the big decisions. But I never really asked my team what they thought and if they even liked what we were doing at all. That lack of understanding of the value a team can bring cost Chop Dawg millions in potential earnings.

Julia Hartz, the cofounder and CEO of Eventbrite, is the

opposite person of who I was in the way that she empowers her team.

Julia found that it's her *team's* love for the company and the people they work with that keeps them productive. According to Julia, the best way to build team loyalty is through empowerment. She gives her team true ownership over decisions and projects. In an essay she wrote on The Muse, she is quite candid about how empowerment doesn't just come out of thin air. Feelings of ownership come from within, and as a founder, it can take a lot of restraint to not be a micromanager.

Julia writes:

> *"At Eventbrite, we call this the "Make it Happen Spirit." But know that no amount of verbiage will effectively make people fully understand ownership. As the person in charge, you need to delegate responsibilities and trust that people can complete them (without any micromanaging). This not only creates an enthusiastic team willing to go the extra mile to support you, but it also clears up room in your schedule to actually, you know, manage."*[1]

---

1   "3 Leadership Lessons Everyone Can Take From This Startup Founder's Success Story." https://www.themuse.com/advice/3-leadership-lessons-everyone-can-take-from-this-startup-founders-success-story

The PiperWai founders also know what's up when it comes to building loyalty and a collective sense of empowerment. Everyone on their team is united by the quality of their product and strives to bring it to as many hands as possible. Because their deodorant is healthy for people and they are 100 percent behind the recipe, everyone feels a strong connection to what they're doing. It's exceedingly rare that your team can all feel genuine connections to the shared mission of a business and then spread that mentality to your own customer base. They're preventing people from using deodorants that are full of chemicals and directing them to a truly good alternative. That's a mission that's easy to get behind, especially with two passionate cofounders at the helm who care about their team.

THAT EGO SHIELD ALSO MAKES EVERYTHING FEEL MAGNIFIED. BE CAREFUL WITH THAT

I failed to realize how little my team was being properly utilized. As I am sure many of you have noticed over the years, the media glamorize the individual founder(s). They fail to see that in reality, they are the face of company, but they are not the ones who do everything. A successful company is the collective work of the whole team. The other reality is that it's the founder who provides the direction. You shouldn't be a leader to feel like the "boss." It's your job to set the course, work with your people to best utilize their inner capabilities, and make sure that everything is on course. You can truly inspire everyone on your team to make contributions to your business and to themselves. Every person on the team should feel like a leader of *change*.

The reality is this: leaders create leaders. The best teams on the planet are the ones that work together, communicate, and function as one horde, and even when facing a setback, remain optimistic and confident that, together, they'll be able to get back on track and move mountains. The reason that Chop Dawg has lasted a decade isn't because of me but because of the fact that we have a plethora of leaders at Chop Dawg who accept and thrive off accountability and team efforts. We're a collective group of leaders, all unified under one goal, one mindset, one mission: to give the best service possible to our clients.

But how does this happen? What makes the team flourish? How does leadership get instilled in everyone? How do you get an entire company of individuals to think with one shared goal?

Anita Roddick was the founder of the Body Shop, a cosmetics company that produces natural beauty products. She was widely known as one of the pioneers of ethical consumerism—the Body Shop was one of the first companies to prohibit the use of ingredients tested on animals—and she was one of the first leaders to promote fair trade with developing countries. She sadly passed away back in 2007, but Dame Anita's (she was knighted!) powerful words on leadership have truly stuck with me:

"What I have learned is that people become motivated when you guide them to the source of their own power and when you make heroes out of employees who personify what you want to see in the organization."

Too many people who start businesses immediately jump to the title of founder/CEO without having anything to back it up. The founder/CEO of *what?* Titles are meaningless; it doesn't matter what you are, the only thing that matters are the results. There is a reason I call myself a passionate student of entrepreneurship over the label "entrepreneur" itself; titles mean nothing, actions mean everything. Rather than getting caught up in your own power, help others discover their own and you'll become more powerful yourself. When you help your team each discover their unique abilities, they learn to decide what they want to do to really lead the charge.

Whether you're a brand-new startup founder or run a company with five hundred people, you can encourage each person on your team to tap into the best version of themselves. Even if you are the sole proprietor, you can do this for yourself and for the people whom you outsource your work to. If you want to be a leader, that means realizing your sole job is to make other leaders. Teach others the way to think; act; remain cool, calm, and collected in times of hardship; and always give value over anything else. That is the code, the DNA of what makes a leader tick.

THE CHIEF ACCOUNTABILITY OFFICER

With both Subtle and the client that fired us, there was no accountability until it was too late. There was a clear flaw in the DNA of our operations, and it was me. I just didn't know how to keep my team accountable. Not yet. There needs to always be someone at a company, especially an infant operation, who keeps the mission on course and makes sure deadlines are met and that everyone is doing what they need to be doing. That individual instills the charisma, personality, and work ethic that a company should be striving for.

If I had to create a more specific job for myself rather than just calling myself the CEO, it would be *chief accountability officer*. This means being responsible, not passing the buck, and leading by example. If you're late to meetings, be on time yourself to teach others that you aren't all talk but that you practice what you preach. How can you breed accountability without being accountable yourself? I think the most important thing of all when it comes to accountability is to encourage honesty—no one should ever be afraid to tell you that something isn't going to plan. The sooner you know something is going wrong, the sooner you have the opportunity to fix it.

THERE IS THIS BELIEF IN ENTREPRENEURSHIP THAT A+ PLAYERS WILL ATTRACT OTHER A+ PLAYERS, BUT B+ AND LOWER WILL ATTRACT ONLY LOWER-GRADED PLAYERS

It is similar to creating a basketball roster in the NBA: superstars want to play with other superstars as they elevate their game, while mid-tier players and lazy veterans want whatever team will give them the most slack so they can collect their paycheck and go home. There is a reason why LeBron James never entertained the idea of joining a team like the Sacramento Kings (sorry, Kings fans). You never get to superstar level alone. You need a team that can push *you*, make you better, and instill the critical philosophies needed to see real, tangible results.

Sometimes you just end up making the wrong hire, too. This will happen, whether it is a founder, colleague, executive, employee, vendor, or contractor. Maybe this person makes others on the team feel small, or maybe they are just not right for the job; either way, you need to cut the wrong hire out sooner rather than later, because the impact ends up having a ripple effect on the rest of the business. Bad hires will eventually happen for any company. It's happened to me. Learn to not let them fester. Bad team members are similar to a cancer in the body. Do not let the cancer cells spread. Address the problem while it is fixable, before it becomes incurable. And for all you employees out there, if this is hitting a little too close to home, maybe it's time to reevaluate yourself and your job. Refer back to Chapter 4: "Self-Awareness."

Phil Kennard had some thoughts about this very issue when considering hires at Futurestay. He pointed out that "with small companies, every hire is going to become a large percentage of your workforce. If you have, say, four existing team members, one new hire is now going to comprise 20 percent of your workforce." The importance of building a company culture early on cannot be overstated! Toxic culture can kill a company. If you do make a misjudgment, you must be quick to remove the toxic person from the team.

Never be slow to fire someone due to cultural reasons, Phil advises. But also be open to nurturing those who have a skill gap.

Skills can be gained, and people become better at their jobs over time with good training. But a poor fundamental attitude and work ethic is something that cannot. Sometimes you'll have people who work for you who were incredible team assets that now need to move on. We have lost a few key people at Chop Dawg in the decade we've been around, and it is stressful at the time it happens. But when you are dealt those blows, you can switch roles around, bring on a replacement, or take on the work yourself. We've turned the occasional turnovers from challenges into opportunities.

LEADERSHIP MEANS ALWAYS ENSURING EVERYONE IS ALIGNED UNDER THE SAME COMPANY OBJECTIVES, WHILE RESPECTING EACH PERSON'S APPROACH TO GETTING THE JOB DONE

It sounds like common sense, but when you treat individuals like the adults that they are, guess what? They will probably act more like the adults that they are. Micromanaging cultures do not need to exist unless you let them exist.

Sure, not every team member at your company will be an equity shareholder or cofounder, but one thing you need to remember is, the best teams have a shared interest in achieving the common objective. When the common objective isn't followed and everyone is working on their own things, you don't have much of a team anymore. You know the saying that a rising tide raises all boats? Well, a falling tide will lower all boats.

Phil pointed out the issues that he has faced with his team working in their own bubbles in the past. I've seen this problem myself with Chop Dawg, because we are a remote team. Phil does believe that people are more productive if

they are working from home on their own stuff. *But* with
collaborative projects, Phil has seen the opposite happen.
From my own experience, I have seen issues, but I'm more
positive on the idea of people working mostly remotely.
I have found that this can be solved by having the team
come together at least a few times a year. That way, all of
my team members know one another personally and have
that chemistry that allows them to be collaborative while
working remotely.

FOR YEARS, I WAS EMBARRASSED BY MY FAILURES AND WANTED TO HIDE MY VULNERABILITIES

Do you think the best entrepreneurs on the planet don't
have bad days?

Look at Phil Knight, the founder of Nike, if you really want
to know what it's like to have a bad day. His competitors
strategically had the United States government suing him,
trying to put him out of business. Worse, Nike was running
low on cash at the same time. If he hadn't beaten the government, Nike as you know it would not exist today. That
famous check mark swoosh—it wouldn't exist. Imagine a
world without Nike. It is impossible because it is so deeply
ingrained in our pop culture and sports.

Phil Knight has been vocal about the countless sleepless
nights he had, the stress he went through, and his fear that

his dream of creating the best running shoe on the planet would come crashing down on him. He had to create an entire market himself, deal with internal sabotage and betrayals, and battle it out with one of the other largest companies on the globe: Adidas. He documents this entire time of Nike's history in his autobiography, *Shoe Dog* (which, in full disclosure, is perhaps one of my favorite books of all time). Nike is still around today, a multibillion-dollar company and one of the most notable brands in existence, with perhaps the most recognizable logo in all the world. Phil Knight persevered.

Leadership is about being real with others and yourself, for the greater good of becoming better. Not acknowledging your weaknesses is not a strength—it's a weakness itself. Never feel ashamed to ask for help. The more I am open about my vulnerabilities, the more people I can find who can help me, and the more quickly I can turn liabilities into strengths.

One thing this has helped with is the quality of my outsourcing.

When you hear about outsourcing, it's usually focused on hiring foreign teams. But I think of good outsourcing as building a lifetime support network for myself. I don't "outsource"; I partner up. These are individuals I can not only depend on but also trust for feedback, guidance, expertise, and information. Again, leadership isn't all about you. It's about how you can connect people together to form your collective. Even if you are sole proprietor, you need to have people you count on for the expertise you lack.

When we make big decisions at Chop Dawg, it is now almost always a team effort. While sometimes I need to be the decision maker (the buck still stops with me), it's always a discussion, because the fact is that I'm only really good at two or three things. I need a collective behind me to help me with everything else that I'm not good at.

WHEN YOU HEAR THE NAME BENJAMIN FRANKLIN, DO YOU THINK OF HIM AS SOMEONE WHO WAS SELFLESS OR SELFISH?

Benjamin Franklin accomplished remarkable things in his lifetime, such as establishing the University of Pennsylvania; being the first US postmaster general; helping draft the US Declaration of Independence; inventing the lightning rod, the odometer, and the Pennsylvania stovetop; and the list goes on.

Even his charitable contributions are still impacting people today. Upon his death, Benjamin Franklin left Philadelphia and Boston £2,000 (with one hitch: that it couldn't be touched for one hundred years and couldn't be entirely used before two hundred years were up). Of course, the interest accumulated on the money exponentially grew to be worth millions in today's value. That £2,000 is now used to improve the two cities, give children scholarships to universities, and even help build and operate Philadelphia's Franklin Institute museum.

Would you consider Mr. Franklin to be selfless or selfish? Well, what if I told you that he was selfish with most of his accomplishments and that this was actually a good thing for the rest of us?

It is well-documented that Benjamin Franklin had poor eyesight over his life and that his vision continued to deteriorate as he aged. This frustrated him to no end, and he used this as motivation to create what at the time he called double-spectacles, which contained on the bottom the glass from his reading glasses, and on the top, the glass from his long-distance glasses. These would be known as bifocals, one of Benjamin's most famous inventions in his lifetime. Most famous paintings of Benjamin feature him in those famous circular spectacles.

Here is the thing: Benjamin Franklin didn't invent the bifocals for anyone else but *himself* initially. He did it with selfish intent. But he eventually identified that others shared the same pain point and channeled his selfish motive into something that impacted thousands of lives for the better. He turned selfishness into selflessness.

I think that too many people have demonized the term "selfishness," tying it to words such as "manipulation," "theft," "greed," and "stealing," while failing to see the benefits that being selfish can bring. Selfishness is, in many ways, the originator of great companies, products, and services. The founder starts something based on their own needs, understanding afterward that others will share the same pain point and be willing to offer compensation for that solution. That is entrepreneurship at its most basic, fundamental level. Some of the best ideas on the planet were born because of someone being "greedy" or "focusing on themselves over others," who turned their idea into solving real problems and creating opportunities and value for others. And isn't identifying a problem, solving it, and helping others with this solution the most perfect example of being a leader?

THERE'S SO MUCH VALUE IN AN HONEST RELATIONSHIP BETWEEN THE BUSINESS AND THE CUSTOMER

Lemonade is an insurance company that is also a certified B Corp, which means that doing social good is literally incorporated into its business model. Their entire claims process is handled by an AI insurance claims specialist that can make decisions quickly based on the most honest outcomes available. Lemonade can now honestly demonstrate that they can approve an insurance claim in as little as three seconds. They also have eighteen antifraud algorithms to determine honesty. This process is mutually beneficial for both sides and encourages honesty. By being better at detecting honesty than a human can and doing a quicker job at it, customers benefit from having a much easier and more fair claims process.

Customers must sign an honesty pledge before making a claim, which sets them up to be more honest from the get-go. This policy comes from research that was conducted by Dan Ariely, who is currently Lemonade's chief behavioral officer. This honesty benefits the customers, because only the people who need their money the most will get serviced, and there will be enough to go around to satisfy legitimate claims from homeowners and renters. And by keeping an honesty pledge of its own, Lemonade donates any remaining unclaimed money for the year to charity.

LET'S REVIEW THE QUALITIES OF BEING A LEADER HIGHLIGHTED IN THIS CHAPTER

Leaders come in many forms, but there are universal qualities. Leadership can be singular, plural, a team effort, a company-wide initiative, or simply a quick conversation where you serve as a mentor or role model to someone. Approach leadership in the way that works for you. I can be boisterous, I can have my head in the clouds, and I can get down to brass tacks. But your approach may be different. If you and others are getting to your common goal, if you can drive change and inspire others to work with you, then you're a leader.

1. Never overpromise and underdeliver. Be transparent and honest with what can get done. If you overdeliver, that's a bonus. Turn overdelivering into your norm.

2. Leadership is not about controlling others. It's helping those who want to be led find their strengths and pursue a common objective. As a leader, you need to keep everyone on course until the common objective has been completed or it's no longer relevant.

3. Be observant. Sniff out opportunities and never settle. It's up to you to make sure everyone who is needed gets to keep their jobs.

4. Have the courage to speak up when the direction needs to be changed, but make it an inclusive process. Don't use your ego as a shield; listen and be open to disagreement.

5. It's your job to keep the accountability going. You should see from a mile away if things aren't moving forward.

6. Don't hide your vulnerabilities. In fact, showing your vulnerabilities can help you find good new opportunities with good people.

7. You can't be good at everything, so having a strong network of people who have your back will put you at a great advantage. Work with your strengths, and don't bother doing the things you stink at. Get good people

to fill those roles, and remember, they don't all have to work for you.

8. Leaders make leaders. You lead by example, by what you say, by how you interact with others. Pay attention to these details with yourself.

These are some of the qualities that I've been able to acquire over the years. There are still many improvements I need to make, and I'm always learning. As I'll bring up later in the book, developing a reliable process is what helps good leadership keep it going. It also takes a keen ability to think in the short term and the long term at once. We'll be going over this power in the next chapter.

CHAPTER 7

SHORT-TERM AND LONG-TERM THINKING

During my time chatting with the PiperWai founders, Jess Edelstein brought up a mantra she'd picked up from other entrepreneurs that kept her going through the difficult work that would make most wantrepreneurs want to quit.

"Live a few years like everybody else won't so you can live the rest of your life like everyone else can't."

It's hard to be an entrepreneur when you're in your twenties and your peers all seem like they are having so much more fun and freedom. But this is an illusion. It is one powerful illusion, though.

This mantra encapsulates the long-term mindset.

It's hard to sustain motivation, and it's easy to get jealous of others. But jealousy is a really unproductive emotion.

In 2012, when all the news stories were starting to come out about entrepreneurs raising enormous amounts of money from investors or making multimillion-dollar exits, it infuriated me. It seemed like they were instantly becoming much more accomplished in the span of a few months than I had been in my first three years. It had been a while since I had been covered in the media, and I couldn't stand feeling like I was now "irrelevant." I was jealous and spent much more time focusing on that than making any real effort to appear in the news more.

I had no sense of purpose or direction. I thought that I was already out of my prime, a burned-out former "superstar" (yeah, OK, Josh...). Sure, you can read interviews of nineteen- and twenty-year-old me about how we were on some great crusade to help others, but that was the thin narrative. It wasn't really how I felt. I wasn't going to be explicit about it, but all I wanted was to be rich and famous. Basically, all of those cliché reasons that make thousands want to be an entrepreneur. I was a wantrepreneur, not an entrepreneur.

I was impatient to accomplish anything and everything to get myself to that "better place" I had in my head. Because of this impatience and my lack of experience, I had started to overestimate the amount of progress I could make in a day, in a week, in a month, or even in a year. I never had the patience to commit to one thing, so instead I did a bunch of half-assed things. There was no focus. Once Subtle imploded, I was faced with the reality that jealousy drove me to impatience, and impatience brought me to an empty bank account.

Think about this for a minute: how much have you accomplished in the last week? Now, in a year? OK, now in five years? Ten years?

It's impossible to know what things are going to be like two decades from now, and it's hard to understand why you still need to think this way and then act methodically upon it. Long-term thinking isn't about thinking of something on a one- or five-year scale. It is about thinking over the course of decades or even a lifetime; a goal can take much longer than your own existence to reach.

MOST OF US ARE USED TO SEEING NEW INVENTIONS COMING OUT ON WHAT FEELS LIKE A WEEKLY BASIS

New phones every summer. New technologies that are quickly adopted worldwide. I've seen the spread of high-speed internet from the days of 56K modems to 4G on phones (and as I type this, 5G). I've seen smartphones go through new adaptations and new uses. I've seen the birth of touchscreen devices, virtual reality, augmented reality, AI, high definition. I've seen the rise of remotely working digital-nomad lifestyles. I've seen changes in the way we socially interact, especially in dating culture. (Remember when it was considered creepy to meet someone online? Yet, that is how I met my significant other!) There are so many new norms that we couldn't have comprehended ten years ago.

As a result, we're raised to move and think quickly. Sadly, that means that even though we have all of these gadgets that help us streamline our time, people's standards of time have changed so much that they don't feel any less time-constrained. And now people expect these inventions to come out quickly. But what people don't see is all of the behind-the-scenes work that goes into developing new technologies. Most of what is considered to be new are actually iterations of a much bigger picture. Smartphone technology, for example, has iterated on itself so many times that it's sometimes difficult to conceive anymore just how different our lives were before we had them. We're now at the point of expecting upgrades by the week; we've reached the exponential curve of technological growth. And now the previously awe-inspiring technology has become the standard. Candidly, it has become underappreciated and taken for granted by the masses.

It really dawned on me the other day how so many people

have *adjusted* to using their smartphones as a way of life. More and more people are exhibiting smartphone-dependent behavior. I think the various upgrades we have seen since 2008 are easy to take for granted because they're more iterations of the technology than anything earth-shattering like the original iPhone.

Let's think about this now from an empathy perspective.

If the smartphone has been a companion in your life for longer than you can remember, is it really possible to know what living without one feels like anymore? A new app that comes out that shakes up the way we do something just feels a little bit *expected*, doesn't it?

I'm borderline between being a millennial and a Generation Z (or iGeneration). There was barely a time when I was growing up that the internet wasn't a standard part of daily life. I can remember life before having a computer... but barely. But the dawn of iPhone was an earth-shattering moment for me. Had I been an adult in, say, 2000, I think my perspective would be much different today.

My perspective is tuned a little differently because smartphones were not a part of my childhood. Smartphones really came to be around the time I became an entrepreneur—at least the modern adaption we as consumers are used to today. I sometimes wonder what I would be like if I had grown up with smartphones. What's even more interesting to me is, as I age, what is going to be the next big thing that changes lives that I will be experiencing for the first time as a full-grown adult? The game is always changing, and I'm sure it'll become more unpredictable the more we know. I have more questions than answers at this point, but I would say that my thinking now is mostly in ten-year increments.

I was recently chatting about long-term thinking with my good friend John Gavigan, who is the chief operating officer of SomaDetect and formerly the chief executive officer of 43North. This startup works with farmers to provide them with real-time analytics of their cows' milk quality and health. Giving farmers these insights allows them to make more informed decisions on how best to take care of their cows. That greatly benefits the cows and also the people who drink their milk. People will be consuming healthier and more nutritious dairy, and the cows will be healthier. And before that, 43North helped provide millions to promising startups and technologies under one stipulation: they must work out of Buffalo, New York, for a year. In return, he would not only help these promising initiatives flourish but also help grow the Buffalo startup and technological ecosystem.

John is a very mission-driven entrepreneur who operates mission-driven companies. So I was not surprised by just how astounded he is by the current technological revolution that humanity is just at the cusp of. John grew up without cell phones or the internet, so he has witnessed firsthand the ways that human lives have been transformed in such a short time.

JOHN IS ABSOLUTELY CONVINCED THAT WE ARE LIVING IN THE MOST FASCINATING TIME OF HUMAN HISTORY

Thinking back to natural selection—and how technology can completely change the rules of nature—John believes that we are at the dawn of a new species (and we're not even referring to the technological advancement called CRISPR either). He admitted to me that he couldn't have possibly predicted our current technological landscape back in 1995. So thinking about that, can we honestly predict what life will be like in 2030? I admit I cannot. And John admits that he can't either, but, boy, does John want to be around when the future does unfold.

John isn't going to just be watching the change unfold; he's going to be a part of it.

Truly game-changing visions take time to form in individual lifetimes. Take James Dyson, the inventor of the breakthrough Dyson vacuum cleaner.

Back in 1974, James Dyson had really had it up to here with

the Hoover Junior vacuum cleaner he had just bought. It always seemed like the bags were clogging up quickly and losing suction. James would try to empty the bag to get the suction back, but this would have no effect. The vacuum remained clogged. When he inspected the bag further, he noticed a layer of dust. This dust was clogging the material mesh, and so the bag was unusable. Out of this frustration, he sought a new way to suck the dirt without having to buy new bags over and over again.

He had observed cyclonic separation as a method of collecting dirt, dust, and debris at his local sawmill. Cyclonic separation removes particulates from an air, gas, or liquid stream without the use of filters, through vortex separation. James was enthralled by the process of removing dust and particulates without needing a bag. Because he knew the sawmill used this type of equipment, he began to investigate the sawmill at night and take measurements of its device. The question was, how could he take a process that only industrial businesses were using and turn it into a consumer vacuum cleaner?

That would turn out to be an arduously long journey.

He first constructed a cardboard-and-Scotch-tape model in his house, connected it to his Hoover with its bag removed, and found it worked well enough to validate his idea! But James had to develop 5,127 prototype designs between 1979 and 1984 to get any attention at all. The traditional vacuum cleaner companies in the UK and the United States were not receptive, because his prototype couldn't possibly win over the vacuum bag market. This market was worth about $500 million at the time. But James was undeterred.

In 1985, he finally found a company that was interested in licensing his design...in Japan. He was able to finally launch his first full-fledged product, the "G-Force" cleaner. Being able to sell in Japan provided the income that he needed to eventually set up his own manufacturing company in 1991.

Once James could manufacture and sell his vacuum on his own terms, that was really the moment when he set himself up for the insane growth in customers that Dyson ended up having. He leveraged the freedom he had made for himself by creating his own breakthrough TV advertising campaign that emphasized the benefits of the product rather than just the features—benefits that no other rival could beat. Fast-forward to 2001, and his best-selling DC01 model made up 47 percent of the upright vacuum cleaner market in the UK.

While the Dyson Dual Cyclone became the fastest-selling vacuum cleaner ever made in the UK, and eventually outsold every manufacturer and distributor that rejected it, it was a long road to that point. James Dyson will tell you himself that no success is truly overnight. While his fans may have seen the product come out of the blue through advertising, the journey for James himself was anything but easy.

LOOK FOR PATTERNS IN THE MOMENTS OF CREATIVE DESTRUCTION BECAUSE NOTHING LASTS FOREVER

Going back to chapter 2 for a second, let's review creative destruction.

Creative destruction happens when an industry that once thrived is obliterated due to some innovation, or even an entirely new industry, that renders the previous industry's existence suddenly useless. For example, piano makers thrived when there was no such thing as the electric keyboard. Pianos also used to be considered household entertainment, before the radio and before television. Once electric keyboards and other forms of entertainment took over the daily lives of people, piano makers saw their industry whittled down to size. I bet many of those poor piano makers never got the memo that they were going to be "downgraded" to a niche business.

You can see these massive shifts time and time again throughout history. They're hard to detect when they are happening. A lot of what we know now is only based on hindsight.

From local trade jobs that were swallowed by factories, to the factory jobs that were taken over by human-led automation, to the fully automated jobs eventually taking over everything. At the heart of each change within the fall of an industry lies consumer demand. It's up to businesses to interpret the changing tides of opinion and desire and cater to them. The long-term thinkers who are quick on their feet realize the opportunities before they are ever spoken of on the news. They are able to not only understand the tides of opinion and desire; they are the ones creating these ripples in the first place.

There are textbook examples of companies thinking this way, too. Remember the iPod? Apple could have decided not to pursue the iPhone, out of fear of cannibalizing one of their most popular, profitable products. Because today, only one type of iPod still exists: the iPod Touch, which is essentially an iPhone without the phone capabilities. iPods, for all intents and purposes, are no more. The consumer decided that an iPod is no longer necessary, thanks to the existence of the iPhone.

To survive creative destruction really takes an understanding of *what* kind of business you are in.

I was recently reading an article from the *Harvard Business Review* titled, "What Business Are You In? Classic Advice from Theodore Levitt." Theodore Levitt was born in Vollmerz, Germany, in 1925. After fleeing the rise of Nazism and immigrating to the United States, he earned a doctorate in economics and eventually joined the faculty of the Harvard Business School. Here's an excerpt from Levitt's transcendent 1960 essay, "Marketing Myopia":

> *Every major industry was once a growth industry. But some that are now riding a wave of growth enthusiasm are very much in the shadow of decline. Others that are thought of as seasoned growth industries have actually stopped growing. In every case, the reason growth is threatened, slowed, or stopped is not because the market is saturated. It is because there has been a failure of management...*

> *The railroads did not stop growing because the need for passenger and freight transportation declined. That grew. The railroads are in trouble today not because that need was filled by others (cars, trucks, airplanes, and even telephones) but because it was not filled by the railroads themselves. They let others take customers away from them because they assumed themselves to be in the railroad business rather than in the transportation business. The reason they defined their industry incorrectly was that they were railroad-oriented instead of*

transportation-oriented; they were product-oriented
instead of customer-oriented.2

With progress comes a race for innovation, and it is up to you as a business owner to be on the front lines. That's why it's imperative to ask yourself whether you're in business to serve your customer, or if you're around to serve your industry. For example, look at how companies like Ford are adapting to the changing transportation industry. Rather than simply relegating themselves to the auto industry, they are not making the same mistake as the railroads and are serving the emerging multimodal transportation needs of people today. Ford is approaching this from multiple angles, such as getting into the rideshare industry by acquiring Chariot in 2016. Chariot itself started out as a shuttle service in 2014 for San Francisco residents who wanted something between a bus and an Uber. As the transportation business shifts in many new directions, Ford is heading the charge in all of them.

IN THE SHORT TERM, MANY PEOPLE LIKE TO HAVE SOMETHING TO DO. IN THE LONG TERM, THEY HOPE TO CREATE MEANING IN WHAT THEY DO

Before Futurestay, Phil Kennard had started a typical IT consulting business. He had a skill for programming, and it felt like the logical way to apply that skill. And the

---

2   Levitt, T. (1960). "Marketing Myopia," *Harvard Business Review.*

business did well. Over the first few years, they acquired high-paying enterprise clients and grew to five full-time employees. However, something was missing for Phil. While he was able to live a comfortable lifestyle, he never felt like he was really achieving anything beyond making money and satisfying clients. Life felt like a high-powered hamster wheel.

Things really changed for him when he had a revelatory discussion with his friend (and eventual cofounder) Jon Fabio one night.

Jon, who was also operating a similar consulting business, but in the marketing space, asked him, "Would you be happy if you doubled your business?" Phil balked. "Um...I would dislike what I do even more than now. Scaling is the opposite of what I want!"

That realization sparked Phil to take a completely different approach to his life. He always knew that he had a skill for creating cool things out of code, but the way he was applying that skill felt totally wrong now. He didn't feel like the true creator that he wanted to be. If his goal was just growth, he could have continued with his IT business. But that obviously would have made him miserable in the long run.

Eyes opened, Phil started poking around during his free

time while operating his IT business. The idea for Futurestay itself sprouted almost organically. He was chatting with some of his friends one night, and they started talking about the difficulties in finding short-term renters. It blew his mind that there wasn't anything out there for small- and medium-size companies to market their rentals more efficiently.

Futurestay would never have been born had Jon and Phil not questioned their work. In the grand scheme of things, their contributions felt meaningless. Ultimately, they made the decision to stop working on anything that didn't provide them with a feeling of purpose. They kept running their respective businesses while building out Futurestay, but they were determined to put any hours they could spare to forge their new path. If you talk to either entrepreneur today, they'll both smile at the fact that they never have to look back at their previous lives, and they love what they are doing now.

You may be at the same crossroads as Phil and Jon. While you may feel hesitant about making the pivot from something that feels comfortable, and you're making money, it's a necessary step. The longer you wait to acknowledge this, the harder it'll be to make the change.

LET'S GO BACK TO THE STORY OF JOHN ACCARDI GETTING HIS COMPANY, ACCARDI PRODUCTS, OFF THE GROUND

When John became an entrepreneur after dropping out of graduate school, he didn't have a product that he was committed to selling. More than anything, he was enthralled by the idea of selling products online. So, over the next two years, he experimented selling many different kinds of products. However, these products largely failed to really make any sales. He was able to keep his resolve and he always enjoyed the process of coming up with a product to sell, but he was also beginning to waver after two years of no momentum.

He emphasized in our talk that even with that mental stress, he just couldn't let go of that *pure excitement* he had to sell products online.

Yes, those two years of almost no sales was a trying time for his self-esteem, and he questioned his future often. But he couldn't abandon the dream—not yet.

And then came his first taste of success.

He decided one Easter that he was going to sell baskets online, something not many sellers were doing yet. He just had a feeling this might work. While he didn't have any real expectations of making sales, he was shocked when he saw that he made $1,500 on his first day of selling the baskets. Looking back, that sales figure seems very small to him now. It was also one of the most special moments of his entrepreneurial career so far. He'd reached nirvana. He'd had his taste of success.

This taste of success shifted his resolve into full gear. It was another month of very slow sales, and it spurred him on for another four months before he landed on a product that would make consistent sales. Those four months were spent vigorously testing new images, tweaking listing descriptions, and coming up with new product SKUs. Even after that first taste, there was still a lot of work to be done, but John kept riding the wave that he had created.

This really goes back to what I wrote about in chapter 3—entrepreneurs have to experiment to find their own recipe for success. But this takes having the resolve to get through the disappointments, keep your enthusiasm high, and keep experimenting.

BUT WHAT ABOUT WHEN THE CURVEBALLS COME ABOUT? THE KIND THAT CAN IMMEDIATELY TURN YOUR LIFE INTO A CHAOTIC MESS?

It doesn't matter if you are a small business, mobile app, service, or the size of a *Fortune* 500 company; there is always that possibility of bad news lurking around the corner that can change the course of your life in an instant. How you deal with it can make all the difference in the world.

Take getting suddenly sued, which happens way more often than any entrepreneur would care to admit.

Neil Patel has had a storied career as a marketing entrepreneur. As the cofounder of Crazy Egg, Hello Bar, and Kissmetrics, he has provided thousands of marketers with invaluable tools that have helped make them a lot of money. I consider him to be one of the content marketing pioneers. You can create multiple novels out of the free valuable content that this guy has written!

But then, one day, completely out of the blue, Kissmetrics was slammed by some of the worst news in Neil's career.

Kissmetrics's goal is to help companies increase their customer lifetime value (LTV)—basically, how many dollars a customer is worth over the full amount of time they are a customer. When it launched, there were no real competitors and the company grew at a healthy pace without too much debt. Neil and his cofounder had been frugal, and they were armed with a large savings account. But then, one day, a really negative article hit *Wired* magazine about the practice of placing undeletable flash cookies on people's computers. Kissmetrics itself was specifically called out in the article, even though flash cookies weren't part of their core technology and they had never used them for anything nefarious. They immediately got rid of the flash cookies, but the damage was done. The story continued to spread like wildfire, and suddenly Neil and his cofounder were slapped with a class action lawsuit.

When Neil was raising some venture capital, he discovered that many investors require the companies they fund to get liability insurance. That would ensure that the company could be protected and compensated in case they got sued. But Neil noticed something in the fine print: the insurance would only pay for an attorney that they assigned themselves. Neil and his cofounder were concerned that the assigned attorney lacked experience in working with internet entrepreneurs. So instead, Neil and his cofounder opted to hire their own lawyer, but that racked up big legal bills that weren't covered. While all this was going on, Neil was still trying to grow a business that was generating bad press.

But luckily, he also learned that people do forgive and forget.

Neil reflects on the epic blog post that details the entire experience:

"One day, you'll have a ton of negative press and dozens of people calling to yell at you each day. And the next

day, everyone forgets. Why? Because someone else will
have the spotlight. Don't try to fight negative PR. Just
keep your mouth shut, and let things pass when possible.
And trust me, they will pass. The more you respond, the
more fuel you add to the fire."

So Neil carried on with business as usual. They were still
able to grow their revenue even as the lawsuit raged on.
Furthermore, Neil made sure that he was the only one
dealing with the lawsuit so that it became almost non-
existent for everyone else, thus allowing the company to
continue to survive and prosper.

Neil also advises:

"Don't look at lawsuits or any obstacles that come your
way as a negative thing. Instead, see them as a learning
experience. They are just roadblocks that you will even-
tually run into as your company gets larger."

Honestly, I still have trouble dealing with these sudden
obstacles when they come. I've had a few of these recently,
including a situation where I thought a client was happy
and they then suddenly asked to cancel their project.
These situations still stress me out to no end when they
occur, but recently I've really come to at least appreciate
the learning experiences. It does truly take experiencing
firsthand the obstacles that feel horrible at the moment

but age much better in the long term. I've been through a few moments when I thought that my company could get into trouble, every one different from the last. I almost always feel blindsided, but slowly I've trained my instincts.

As Mike Tyson says, "Everyone has a plan till they get punched in the mouth."

It's about training your instincts. You can't plan your feelings or reaction to a hypothetical company disaster. Think about what you would do for sure, but the true test of how you actually handle it is when it happens. Over time, you'll have the awareness to know what happened, how it went, and what you learned. So let's be real—I'm still stressed when I get hit with the curveballs. They're almost always different. But I'm not stressed for nearly as long as I used to be, and being grateful for the learning experience really does help.

WHAT I ALSO REALLY THINK INHIBITS THE ABILITY TO TAKE BAD NEWS IN STRIDE IS THE CONSTANT FEAR OF BEING EXPOSED, GETTING YOUR EGO BRUISED

You fear that if your company receives a sudden financial threat, you won't be able to handle it. As a result, you don't prepare yourself to receive bad news, so when it comes, you end up holding up your emotional defenses.

This has happened to me, and it probably will again. However, this doesn't mean that you can't build defenses for yourself so that you can handle bad news better. Building real defenses gives you the abilities you need to handle criticism and bad news well.

One of my favorite quotes is from Seneca, the Roman Stoic philosopher: "A commander never puts such trust in peace that he fails to prepare for a war."

A lot of what makes us feel frustrated, annoyed, or even overly happy is the short-term stuff: short-term stuff we weren't prepared for, mentally, emotionally, or physically. But it doesn't feel like short-term stuff at the time.

Anger is a stupid emotion and is short-term thinking. Sometimes it's an inevitable emotion, but it's not rational, and you aren't going to make good decisions while in the heat of anger. Every moment that something didn't go right for me early in my entrepreneurial career felt like a complete loss of control. I would get mad without offering any solutions. I worked my team and myself to the bone because I really felt like that's what I was supposed to do. Today, after having to deal with the out-of-left-field problems and disappointments, my reactions have changed.

Can you remember what you were upset about a year ago? Probably not. These things take up all of our energy and distract us from accomplishing bigger, more important goals. Once you understand this concept, you can begin to leverage long-term thinking to help you block out the noise.

LONG-TERM THINKING GIVES YOU THE ABILITY TO GROW AT A CAREFUL SCALE

In 1951, John C. Bogle submitted an undergraduate thesis at Princeton University that challenged a previously unquestioned economics assumption.

His study revealed that most mutual funds did not earn any more money than if you just invested in the broad stock market indexes yourself. John found that *even if* you could earn more money from a mutual fund, the management fees eroded any monetary gain. Immediately after graduating Princeton, he was hired by Wellington Management Company. By 1966, he had forged a merger with another company; he became president in 1967, and then CEO in 1970. But the merger ended badly. By 1974, he had been fired. This turned out to be the greatest thing to happen to him.

"The great thing about that mistake," John C. Bogle reflects, "which was shameful and inexcusable and a reflection of immaturity and confidence beyond what the facts justified, was that I learned a lot. And if I had not been fired then, there would not have been a Vanguard."

Yes, you read that right, Vanguard. John would end up creating Vanguard, which for those in the financial industry, is perhaps the biggest disrupter of their space in the last fifty years.

While competitors peddled high-fee funds claiming to "beat the market," he created a low-cost index approach. Competitors called it "Bogle's Folly" and claimed it was "un-American" simply to try to match the performance of the stock market rather than try to beat it. In 1976, Bogle established the First Index Investment Trust (now called the Vanguard 500 Index Fund).

When you put your money into a Vanguard, the magic isn't in your individual contributions. It's in the compound interest of all your contributions over time. The larger your principal becomes based on your contributions, the more it will be able to compound. The more time you give your fund to compound, the larger it will become.

This is how you need to approach your business.

This is also where the difference between having goals and having systems in place becomes especially important.

A goal is wanting to sell a million units; the system is setting up the actual sales and marketing operations you need to be able to sell those million units. Setting up a *system* gives you the process that holds you accountable to accomplish a goal. Simply setting goals is not enough.

Rashmi Sinha is the cofounder and CEO of SlideShare, a platform where people can post their presentations. Since launching SlideShare in 2006, the company has seen massive success and has since been acquired by LinkedIn (and, therefore, Microsoft). It gets about 80 million unique users per month and has about 38 million registered users. Rashmi's daily duties are all about developing partnerships and product strategy, and her success is built around the system she has in place for herself and for her team.

Every morning, Rashmi gets into her office at around nine thirty or ten o'clock and checks her emails first thing. She prioritizes responding to all important emails, but it's also part of her system to make sure that *all* emails are tended to during this ritual, so her mental space for the rest of the day isn't occupied by them.

According to Rashmi, "If I don't [do this], I'm spending my time twice."

How she works with her team is also part of her system. Every Monday morning, she has a scrum meeting with the team. Scrum is a system that is used a lot in software development. It's a system designed for people to break up their work into actions that can be completed within "sprints," or boxes of time. The length of each sprint depends on what the team is working on, but tracking progress is key. Having stand-up meetings is also a backbone of this system; Rashmi describes them as a "rugby huddle." During these stand-ups, everyone on the team has a few minutes to say three things:

1. What did you do last week?
2. What would you like to do today?
3. What do you need from *someone else* in order to get this done?

By holding these fifteen-minute scrum meetings about two to three times per week, Rashmi gets a great overhead view of what is going on with her team. Her system has helped make SlideShare's culture laid-back and productive at the same time.

Is every task you've completed following your long-term system and a contribution to a greater goal you've set? Just like with the Vanguard fund, even the smallest of contributions today starts to add up when it connects with all the other tasks you've completed. It simply requires a system.

DR. NORMAN VINCENT PEALE, MINISTER AND A PROGENITOR OF THE THEORY OF POSITIVE THINKING, ONCE SAID, "SHOOT FOR THE MOON. EVEN IF YOU MISS, YOU'LL LAND AMONG THE STARS"

Whenever I am doing anything, whether it is writing this book, joining someone on a podcast, working with a client, working alongside my team, or giving back to my community, I always ask myself the same question: *Is what I'm doing related to and contributing to the system I set in place for getting Chop Dawg to the moon?*

As founders, we often place the burden of being the sole problem solver upon ourselves. But ideas and problems can span generations; no one person can possibly solve problems of that magnitude. Rather than shooting for the moon ourselves, sometimes we have to first create the system that can facilitate others getting there. Worst case, you might not land on the moon, but even reaching the stars is one hell of an accomplishment (cliché but true).

JIM ROHN ONCE SAID, "YOU AREN'T PAID FOR YOUR TIME, BUT THE VALUE THAT YOU BRING"

Rohn first made his money through direct selling, but he became famous after his local Rotary Club invited him to speak at one of their meetings. This launched him into the memorable part of his career—corporate speaking. While this circuit is flooded now, Rohn found in it a new calling and was able to carry over a lot of the skills that he learned as a direct seller.

And he is absolutely right—the time spent on something doesn't intrinsically create any value. The common equation of time spent to value is a product of the Efficiency Movement, which swept the United States and other industrializing nations in the early twentieth century. We have been on this quest for efficiency as a culture ever since—damn, does it feel good to check off all the boxes! But while we *do* have a lot more free time, we feel like we are *doing less*. I honestly think that's why I gravitate toward sending and responding to emails—it's in my DNA to get that instant gratification from a well-thought-out letter to someone. But what's the purpose? Sending emails is productive when I'm doing outreach, but if I'm sending my team a novel's worth of ideas over emails, that sense of actually getting something done is false. I not only wasted my own time but also my team's time for having to read the whole thing in the first place.

The moral of the story is, don't waste your time with busywork, or what we affectionately referred to previously as mental masturbation. Put your efforts toward accomplishing long-term goals that can provide you and others with tangible value.

THAT'S WHY SHARING AND PASSING ALONG BENEFITS TO OTHERS IS SO IMPORTANT TO YOUR LONG-TERM ENTREPRENEURSHIP GOALS

By the mid-nineteenth century, the Colorado gold rush was starting to take shape. Clara Brown, a former slave, would be one of the first entrepreneurs who would accrue a lot of wealth from it.

Clara was hired as a maid and cook by a family heading westward. This eventually led to a job as a cook on a wagon train, a difficult job on a hot, harrowing cross-country journey, especially because of the men who complained about a black woman traveling with them. But Clara was incredibly observant and identified the tide of gold miners moving up to the mountains of Colorado. She followed that tide and opened up a laundromat in the town of Central City to serve the miners. Her business skyrocketed once she found a business partner, and she began investing in land around the mines. She eventually owned sixteen lots in Denver, seven houses in Central City, and property around other mining towns.

But Clara didn't just keep everything for herself. Her own home became a hospital and general refuge for those sick or in poverty; people lovingly referred to her as "Aunt Clara." She also used her investment returns to buy the freedom of slaves in her family. Once slavery was fully abolished, she found others in her family and helped them properly settle by buying them land and housing. In 1879, she helped a group of former slaves build a community and farm.

By the time she turned eighty, Clara's funds were depleted due to all of the contributions she had made, her efforts to find her family, and being cheated by real estate agents. But despite the sad final outcome, Clara Brown's journey from slavery to entrepreneurship was incredible, and her contributions were lasting. By empowering others throughout her life, she extended her impact well beyond herself.

WHEN THINKING ABOUT CREATING TRUE VALUE, ASK YOURSELF THIS: "DO I HAVE A GROWTH MINDSET OR A FIXED MINDSET?"

Around thirty years ago, renowned psychologist Dr. Carol Dweck and her team became interested in students' attitudes about failure. They noticed that some students rebounded, while others seemed devastated by even the smallest setbacks. You can read more about this research in her 2006 book, *Mindset: The New Psychology of Success.*

From their study, Dr. Dweck and her team could place people into two categories:

1. Those who have a "fixed" theory of intelligence (fixed mindset). Fixed-mindset people tend to think

that whatever abilities they have will go unchanged, no matter what they do. There's no room for self-improvement or new ideas with this mindset.

2. Those who believe that they are in control of their success through learning and hard work. In other words, they were open to "growth" opportunities in intelligence (growth mindset). There are countless opportunities to grow and learn. The best of entrepreneurs exhibit the growth mindset.

The interesting part was that Dr. Dweck's students weren't necessarily aware of their proclivities toward a growth or fixed mindset. However, she and her team discerned from behaviors such as fearing failure that some people leaned toward fixed mindsets, while the growth-minded individuals viewed failure as a learning experience. Those growth-minded students knew they could pick themselves up and apply what they'd learned to the next endeavor.

According to Dr. Dweck:

> *In a fixed mindset students believe their basic abilities, their intelligence, their talents, are just fixed traits. They have a certain amount and that's that, and then their goal becomes to look smart all the time and never look dumb. Growth mindset students understand that their talents and abilities can be developed through effort, good teaching and persistence. They don't nec-*

essarily think everyone's the same or anyone can be
Einstein, but they believe everyone can get smarter if
they work at it.3

This is very important for entrepreneurs to consider because:

1. As an entrepreneur, you need to continue to work hard after a setback.
2. To properly start a company, you can't fear failure.
3. You need to interpret each failure as a learning experience. Your flaws are not something to lament but rather something that you should want to address.
4. You shouldn't want to learn just so you can look smart. No one cares. It's all about your own learning and personal growth.
5. You need to be self-aware enough to constantly learn from your relationships.

Derek Sivers is living proof of the growth mindset at work. Derek started CD Baby (an online CD store for independent musicians) by accident in 1996, when he was selling his own CD on his website and friends asked if he could sell theirs, too. CD Baby became the largest seller of independent records online and brought in over $100 million in sales for more than 150,000 musicians.

---

3   Carol S. Dweck Ph.D, (2006) *Mindset: The New Psychology Of Success.*

The way that Derek sold the company was especially interesting (and compassionate): he transferred the company into a charitable trust for music education and had the trust sell CD Baby to Disc Makers.

Here's what Derek Sivers thinks of the growth versus fixed mindset:

> *"In a fixed mindset, you want to hide your flaws so you're not judged or labeled a failure. In a growth mindset, your flaws are just a TO-DO list of things to improve."*[4]

He's right; we really do run away from our flaws, which I think is just a general human proclivity. But that doesn't mean that we can't improve ourselves.

There's one other thing growth-mindset individuals think about differently compared to fixed-mindset individuals: *money.*

LONG-TERM SUCCESS AND SHORT-TERM DOLLARS

When Ben Chestnut and Dan Kurzius founded their email marketing platform, MailChimp, in 2001, it was not their goal to acquire 14,000 new customers per day. These are the kinds of customer numbers that they have now, but they didn't start out with any such dreams. They certainly

---

4   Sivers, Derek (2014). "Fixed Mindset vs Growth Mindset." https://sivers.org/mindset

did not imagine big venture capital investments or acquisitions either. They also didn't care about being the leaders of their industry or having millions of users and dollars.

Until about 2007, MailChimp remained a quiet side project. They wanted to help their existing web design business clients get better at sending emails to their customers. Their clients had been asking for it, and so Ben unearthed some code that he had made from a failed online greeting card business. When they felt confident that there was really something to MailChimp as a stand-alone business, they decided to go all in. They had realized that in the long-term, they weren't that passionate about web design, even if that business could bring in the short-term dollars.

Going all in with MailChimp had its challenges. By 2007, email marketing was a tough business to get into. Not only were there already Goliaths such as Constant Contact in the email marketing industry, but people were getting sick of all the spam. Email services such as Gmail were starting to react against this spam, and it was getting harder to send out mass emails to customers without getting buried in the spam box. But that didn't matter to the MailChimp founders—they were driven by their belief in email marketing as a solution for small businesses, as they had not been sought out by the Goliaths. They were determined to carve their own way into the industry, even if the real financial gains would be a long time coming.

MailChimp's strategy for the long term was to get close to its customers. Because MailChimp *itself* was a small business, its founders were able to have empathy for what customers really wanted and needed from their email marketing tools. They offered an experience to their customers that was more affordable and intimately tailored to meet their needs.

When venture capitalists showed interest, Ben and Dan continually denied the funds. Today, even with millions of users, they continue to run a bootstrapped business. MailChimp still completely owns itself, and they've been able to accumulate assets even greater than money. They have a lovable brand that stands out, along with a loyal customer base, and they've always made the necessary incremental improvements to satisfy customers, new and old alike. Because they are completely independent of outside investor influence, they have complete ownership of their company and can really work for their customers. My own company, Chop Dawg, adheres to the same formula today.

SO WHEN IS IT SUITABLE TO EXPRESS SHORT-TERM THINKING? HOW CAN YOU MAKE THESE DECISIONS?

I have spent a lot of time in this chapter focusing on the benefits of long-term thinking. However, I also believe there are suitable cases of short-term thinking.

In his 2016 annual letter to his shareholders, Amazon founder Jeff Bezos went through his decision-making process for short-term and long-term thinking. This is a method that can be applied to any organization. He distinguishes decisions between "Type 1" and "Type 2":

1. "Type 2 decisions" are two-way doors that can be reversed. If you make a suboptimal type 2 decision, you can reopen the door and unwind the consequences. Because of this, these decisions can and should be made quickly. As organizations grow, there is a tendency to turn all decisions into type 1s. The end result is slowness and diminished innovation. Most decisions should be made with close to 70 percent of the information needed. Waiting for 90 percent-plus information will slow you down.

2. When consensus is not possible but you have conviction toward a particular direction, "disagree and commit." This means that while you disagree with the decision, you remain committed to a successful outcome. Staying focused on trying to change the team's mind is too slow of an approach.

3. Recognize when an agreement isn't achievable. Sometimes different teams have different objectives and see the world differently. No discussion will change these views. A quick escalation in these scenarios is much better than constant argument, which will lead to exhaustion.

me. Then my cousin Frankie came in and said, "No, you have to tune it first." He taught me how to tune it, and I kept practicing. And I kept practicing. And I put on the Beatle[s] records and I practiced them. And I put on the Rolling Stone[s] records and I practiced them. And I practiced. And I practiced. And it sounded like shit. But I kept practicing. And I practiced. And I practiced. And I practiced. And practiced. Ten thousand hours? Much more than ten thousand hours, many more. I practiced until one day I picked it up and it went...

Cutting off his story, he played a guitar riff that sounded terrible.

I think we would all like to become masterful guitar players in the short term if we could. But that's not the way it works. When you doubt yourself while planning big, it's because you've failed to develop a long-term strategy. We had put ourselves in the position to fail by thinking too short term and learned our lesson.

Don't do that. Otherwise, life will be pretty boring.

CHAPTER 8

ECONOMICS

I started Chop Dawg in 2009, during the lowest point of the Great Recession. As a teenager, I witnessed the Great Recession's impact on my own parents, best friends, and everyone I knew. As I recalled chapter 2, it was a ruthless force that I do not wish on anyone.

The banks too were ailing, so it was tough for entrepreneurs to get credit or loans if they needed financing. Some investors had been ruined by the crash, so there were not nearly as many angel and venture capital investors. Just like that, it became a lot harder to find money to start a business.

There are a few reasons why I was able to get started on a business during the Great Recession:

1. Chop Dawg had zero upstart costs, with no need for any credit to start. No loans, just ten dollars for the domain name. I picked a service that required only my own time and labor in the beginning.

2. I was also selling a service that was at just the right rock-bottom price to fill a need. Local small businesses desperately needed more sales because so many people weren't purchasing as they had been, pre-recession. A website could give these businesses a new way to reach their customers.

3. The timing was just right. From an economic standpoint, the Great Recession was such an opportunity to trailblaze if you were selling the right thing at the right cost.

Since the lows of the recession, entrepreneurs have slowly gained access to more loans and other forms of credit. That's also helped my own business. The more clients who can get low interest loans or funding, the better! But I haven't needed to take out any loans or receive any funding yet. Now would be the time for me to try to acquire that, if I needed it. While the economy is showing positive signs of growth and confidence, the Federal Reserve is slowly raising the interest rates in the money they lend to banks. That rings some alarm bells in my mind.

Think about it: when the banks have less to give and they themselves are paying higher interest, that is passed down to you. Since the crash, the Federal Reserve has kept interest rates artificially low. But now, they're starting to pop back up. I don't know when yet, but I feel the next recession coming. I see the signs—when the interest rate gets too high, economic activity slows down. I've never had to weather a correction or crash before with Chop Dawg, so this should be interesting. I'm preparing now. This year, I'll be celebrating my company's tenth anniversary. Will this also be the harbinger of economic doom?

Right now, two-thirds of American households are desperately scrambling to make ends meet, living paycheck to paycheck. Nearly half of the American population earns too little to live comfortably. So it's not looking good to me—a recession is coming. And running a business is hard enough without the complications of a shaky economy.

So I'm building up my cash reserves so that in the eventuality that we get less client work, we'll be able to weather it. I can still pay my team, and we can plan next steps without worrying about the short term, at least for a while.

I don't mean to start this chapter off so doom and gloom. I'm confident that if you can weather the next economic crash, make the right moves, and study the needs of people who are suffering, there's the potential to make a fortune.

THE COST OF BUSINESS CAN BECOME VERY VOLATILE IF YOU ARE SELLING A COMMODITY

A commodity is a basic good that is interchangeable with other commodities of the same type. In Chop Dawg's case, our web services became interchangeable with our competitors. Later, our app services also became interchangeable with everyone else's work. If what you are selling to your customer doesn't create a unique, lasting value over time, you're offering a commodity. With commodities, it doesn't matter who made it. So don't dismiss the creative spirit within you. Customers who don't feel any kind of personal connection with your product will flock to the cheaper alternative when it rolls around. Sometimes you can adapt your product or service so that it's no longer considered a commodity. Other times, you'll simply need to abandon what you're selling and move on to something else.

That's exactly what Ryan Petersen had to do with his company, OCZ Technology Group. He founded the company in 2002 out of his garage, spending $80,000 of his own money to build and sell dynamic random access memory (DRAM) modules for computers. These memory modules were blazing fast, and Ryan started out with very little competition. But as more and more companies began building DRAM modules of their own, Ryan's product lost its distinctiveness. There is only so much you can do to distinguish one DRAM product from the other. Ryan saw his product become a commodity before his eyes.

Prices went down for DRAM because it was so plentiful. Price became the chief consideration of most customers. Even though they were offering a high-end product, Ryan and his team were suddenly speeding in a race to the bottom. By 2007, they had cut their prices from $200 to $20 per module. High end just couldn't cut it because most customers found OCZ's DRAM indistinguishable from anyone else's.

With their profit margins wiped out, Ryan knew they needed to shift over to an entirely different product. It would need to be a slow phaseout, but there was no going back to the days of selling expensive, high-margin DRAM products.

Ryan determined that their new product would be solid-state drives (SSDs), which you may know as a much faster and durable alternative to traditional computer hard drives. The challenge, of course, was the market for SSDs didn't exist yet. Just like with DRAM, Ryan had to create a market of his own. This transition wouldn't be easy. In fact, this transition would cost OCZ $750,000 of their own money so they could start building out SSDs.

Ryan and his team were smart in amassing a backlog of orders before going to investors. That way, they were able to secure the necessary $15 million to fulfill their backorders because they had the proof that people wanted them. OCZ was able to fully transition out of the commodity realm, and a few years later, after making millions in monthly sales, they were acquired. If OCZ were still on its own today, would it have to make a similar shift? Yes—SSDs were always going to be vulnerable to the same shelf-life issues that came with DRAM before them. But that was OCZ's model—find a product that works, sell it for a while, capitalize on that success, and then innovate.

When your product starts to become a commodity, it's time to think outside of the box. Connect with customers, learn what they want, offer something new, and diversify your revenues.

HEALTHY BUSINESSES ARE ALWAYS OBSESSED WITH THEIR VITALS

Similar to a nurse checking your vitals at the hospital, you don't know how you're doing until you check. I check up on my vitals often.

I have come up with a quick checklist to gauge Chop Dawg's vitals:

1. What is our current value and position in our market? How is our market changing?
2. What is Chop Dawg's cash flow compared to our expenses month to month?
3. If we were to lose all of our business today, how much

runway would we have to keep the lights on and think of our next move?

4. How is the quality of what we are currently producing? What needs to get done, and what is preventing us from completing the necessities?

Let's dive into each of these vitals.

HOW DO YOU ASSESS YOUR VALUE, POSITION, AND THE MARKET THAT YOU'RE IN?

A lot of businesses exist as only a reiteration of an existing product or service. How many times in the early 2010s did you hear that your friends were going to start a Facebook for X, Instagram for X, Uber for X, or Airbnb for X? When a disruptive business shakes things up *and* seems to validate itself quickly through high customer volume, the copycats come swooping in. As Michael Gasiorek said, it's the calling of the herd.

The pioneers in any industry's biggest advantage over the herd is clearly market share. If you aren't a pioneer, it's that much tougher to get and hold on to market share, because you're now fighting for the scraps. It becomes more costly to own a market that has too many players, which is called saturation. Investing too much into your business to gain market share may also end up screwing up your other vitals.

By offering the same experience with maybe one or two tweaks, you fail on the opportunity to create a *legitimate alternative* for people. Creating a legitimate alternative is how you challenge a market, not just enter it. And once you create that legitimate alternative, it'll be good for you to have some competitors of your own to validate your own existence to people.

Creating true alternatives also takes time—take a company like Memphis Meats. Founded by three scientists—Uma Valeti, Nicholas Genovese, and Will Clem—this food technology startup is creating sustainable cultured meat. Cultured meat doesn't just taste and feel just like meat; it processes the stem cells of an animal to create literal meat. It's possible only because of recent advances in biotechnology, so the timing is right for Memphis Meats to provide an alternative to meat that drastically reduces the costs and environmental impact of meat consumption. Memphis Meats is not ready for the market yet, so for now, they're researching ways to lower their cost for production. So far, they have raised more than $17 million in a Series A. Memphis Meats aims to be ready for the market by 2021, by which time they should be educated enough about cultured meats to conjure up enough demand.

By 2021, I'm also sure that Memphis Meats will have many more competitors, despite their head start. But this will actually help out pioneers such as Memphis Meats initially. Customers want something to compare to, especially when they're faced with something new. Memphis Meats will have the advantage with its head start in R&D. And while they are putting up the majority of the cost to open up the cultured meat market, this will also give them top billing for customers. A million cultured meat alternatives could crop up in the next decade, but if Memphis Meats can win out in other qualities besides being the first cultured meat provider, that'll help them become not just a commodity but also a market leader.

THE WARREN BUFFETT "MOAT" METAPHOR

Warren Buffett lives by a set of principles when thinking about his investments. These principles have made him one of the wealthiest individuals in human history. He advises people to look for the companies that have built protective "moats" for themselves.

The moat is a river or channel surrounding a castle, intended to keep out invaders and unwanted people. Warren uses it as a metaphor for a business's protective force, built to prevent possible negative outcomes. Warren looks to invest in companies that aren't vulnerable to market changes, competitors, or outside forces. He looks to invest in companies that have something intangible to protect themselves in the bad times and flourish in the good times—their moats.

What could be some parts of your moat?

1. Trusted relationships with your customers and your personal network over a sustained period.
2. Cutting down costs for the unnecessary and investing in the necessary. Gamble responsibly, and distinguish the difference between gambling and smart investing.
3. Preparing alternative strategies and/or new products in anticipation of changes to people's preferences or market changes. Just because you may get the bulk of your sales from one source doesn't mean that's a lifetime guarantee. As the saying goes, never put all of your eggs in one basket.
4. Challenging the way your company does its operations from time to time.
5. Keeping the company savings account full and letting it grow. That money can protect your company from the bad times.
6. If your product becomes a commodity, make sure you're immediately ready to pivot or move on.

I'm still laying out sections of our company "moat" myself. It's an ongoing process, and it should be. My 2016 epiphany that I wanted to get Chop Dawg out of its comfort zone had a grimmer realization coupled with it:

It wasn't just that we would be stagnant. If I just kept things up as they were, we wouldn't be around in two years.

Twitter, our primary source of leads, was showing early signs of not working for us anymore in late 2016. Our app development service was becoming just another commodity again, in an industry that is now very commodity-focused. With customer expectations of service rising, a demand for lower prices, and overseas development shops improving their services, we needed to offer something distinguishable to build a long-lasting advantage in our market.

I needed to think about *what* it was that we really wanted to do. We were building applications, but for whom and why? What was our true service that went beyond just building apps?

We got closer with our customers to learn why they wanted the technology that we were building for them. Just like Ben and Dan of MailChimp were able to do, we proximity to our customers a priority. We would go beyond just delivering on the service of building an app. Now we were interested in helping businesses figure out the technology they really needed and becoming an extension of their team. We could no longer just develop apps—my team would need to broaden its own expertise. Now that I had a real marketer to work with, we could study new ways to reach brand-new clients.

What I've been delighted to learn is that clients can truly

come from anywhere. Recently, we've gotten much better with our search engine presence. This has actually been a double blessing, because we now have higher-budget leads coming in than Twitter ever offered. I'm thankful for the ongoing erosion of Twitter as our primary source of leads, as it forced me to finally examine our reason for existing. We needed to diversify.

IN THE INVESTMENT WORLD, TO "HEDGE" MEANS TO MITIGATE YOUR DOWNSIDE WHILE MAINTAINING YOUR UPSIDE

You can't be afraid to take risks for the sake of becoming complacent or forgotten as the New Economy passes you by, but you also need to be aware and strategic about mitigating the downsides.

Sir Richard Branson became a successful entrepreneur not just through his willingness to spot opportunities but also for his ability to hedge his bets. When Virgin Airlines opened, it was considered one of the riskiest moves he had ever taken. He saw the opportunity that existed in the airline industry, due to poor standards of customer service, and realized he could leverage his obsession with providing the best customer experience to become a dominant player in the market. But as you could probably guess, airlines are incredibly expensive to start. They require extensive and consistent cash flows to make a profit—you're paying daily for labor, marketing, and legal, along with the fuel, planes, airports, runways, and maintenance.

Sir Richard Branson had multiple things working for him to hedge his risk. For starters, the Virgin brand already had multiple profitable channels. Second, Sir Richard hedged his own risks when making the investment. How so? One of the most expensive parts of the investment was building and paying off these incredibly expensive airplanes.

But Sir Richard had a brilliant idea: come up with an agreement with the airline manufacturers to buy back the airplanes if Virgin should fail in the airline business. Yes, you read that right. This way, Sir Richard and the Virgin brand would get the maximum upside should the airline succeed. If it didn't, the fallout would be dramatically mitigated by having an opt-out built in.

BUT NO MATTER WHAT, THE STRUCTURAL INTEGRITY OF YOUR MOAT IS DETERMINED BY YOUR CASH FLOW MOST OF ALL

Without revenue, you simply don't exist as a business. No one is going to fund or give a loan to a business that doesn't have revenue potential—every dollar you are paid is tied to the value you provide. If you can't pay off your credit cards in full every month, you need to slow down your expenses. Never put your business in a compromising long-term position, like having to pay off a ton of high-interest debt.

Always check your cash vitals and make sure you plan a contingency in case the economy suddenly takes a dip.

I see too many businesses blow up during good economic conditions and quickly become bloated with expenses. They're too quick to go for the big office, the extravagant parties, and the perks. They purchase expenses that don't directly grow the business—they aren't investments, they're just expenses. The materialistic expenses don't bring in more money, build infrastructure, or benefit the well-being of their employees.

Well-funded companies can be victims of their success because they get too excited spending—once growth or revenue falls back, they're stuck.

Take it from Jawbone, which ultimately failed to hold on to its once-significant market share for headsets, fitness trackers, and wireless speakers, despite the fact that it had $930 million in funding during its seventeen years in business. You would think that with that amount of funding, Jawbone could have taken on Fitbit in the wearables market. Its valuation had exceeded $3 billion at one point, but no investor money in the world could have prevented the inevitable: they just weren't profitable, ever.

Worse, even with all that investor money, they could never make a dent in the market share that Fitbit had. If Jawbone had played its cards correctly, they would have gone for an acquisition back when they were hot, rather than doubling down on the investor dollars. But instead, Jawbone got too deep into a risky funding round that resulted in an artificially bloated value that ultimately became its undoing. Other investors started getting wary that the company was raising *too* much money that could never compare to actual revenue. The founders tried to sell off the company in 2016 but couldn't. To this day, they are still being sued by vendors claiming that they owe hundreds of thousands of dollars.

The lesson is, be careful with seeking funding for your company. Just because you can raise a big round doesn't mean your company is healthy, and a successful round today can be the cause for failure tomorrow.

FOR CHOP DAWG, WHAT WAS THE EXPENSE THAT NEARLY KILLED US?

It was the seemingly small recurring expenses for subscription-based services that nearly killed us. At one point, we were paying for far too many subscription-based services that weren't bringing in ROI or being used that much. One month, I saw we owed a few thousand dollars in recurring expenses! So we did an audit on ourselves. We looked into every expense we had, going down the line and determining which subscriptions were really needed and which ones should be relegated to the trash.

We came up with these four questions for each subscription:

1. Will we see any kind of potential ROI from this expense?
2. Does this expense improve our offering in any way?
3. Is our team utilizing this expense to the point that it is critical to operations?
4. Is this expense going on a credit card or being paid with cash?

The money you save from unnecessary expenses should become your emergency fund. For instance, getting sued is more common for businesses than you think—don't forget Neil Patel's story from last chapter.

Finally, really think it through when you're deciding how much to divide up ownership in your company. Profits will need to be reinvested back into the business for a long time, so part of your moat is making sure that all of the owners are putting in their fair share to make the business valuable. Dead weight holding on to equity will crush your business when you need it most, so I will always tell people this: be very wary of whom you offer equity to; don't pick just anyone. And treasure those you do pick. Ask yourself, could your company survive without them, short term and long term? Are these individuals someone you can count on when the times get tough? Are these individuals who will develop a strong company culture?

MANY NEW BUSINESSES WERE BORN OUT OF THE GREAT RECESSION. BUT WHY?

It's pure instinct wrought by years of evolution that, for many humans facing danger, leads to fight or flight. What always pains me is when people automatically decide that there's nothing they can do about a bad economy. They're not thinking about the different products and services needed post-crash versus pre-crash. If you can solve a fresh-out-of-the-recession pain point at the right price, you have a chance of buying into the dip and helping a lot of people in pain at the same time. People still want things during a recession; what matters to them simply changes. What you sell and your own expertise may need to evolve accordingly.

I'm also preparing myself for the next recession by becoming more diversified in my own skills and what I'm willing to put the time in to learn. For example, I have been working toward becoming an expert on the technology that is under the hood of the apps we're making. This is important to me for a variety of reasons, one of them being that the needs of the future are going to be so technology-based that I will eventually fail if I don't understand how it all gets made. Becoming a builder is going to be a prime skillset in the New Economy. You need to become the expert your business needs.

When I spoke with Lisa Wang (the founder of SheWorx),

she emphasized the incredible value of owning your domain expertise.

"A problem that comes up with a lot of nontechnical founders is that they want to outsource all of their tech. Think about your domain expertise: are you an expert of your industry? You need to understand the technology that you are building inside and out. It's the same way that a restaurant run by a chef has a specific DNA."

She's absolutely right. If you outsource everything, without having an intimate understanding of what powers your business, you're missing out on another currency that will become more and more valuable.

BUT EVEN WITH CASH RESERVES, VALIDATION, AND A MOAT, CHOP DAWG STILL LACKED A FIRM *PROCESS* FOR GETTING THINGS DONE

Without having operations for making sure we all got paid faster, ensuring projects were done on time, and making sales, Chop Dawg was still vulnerable. I used the cash reserves I had to bring in talent who understood process, while being a great cultural fit. I hired people who can focus not just on the immediate client projects, but who can also work on things that build up our cash reserves and create automated funnels so that recurring business isn't dependent on any specific individual.

During the good times, even as you're reaping the rewards and opportunities, you need to ask yourself how to prepare for the bad. During those bad times, you need to ensure you are focusing on the things that really matter when entrepreneurship isn't considered "sexy," and set yourself up to reap the rewards the good times will bring to you.

That's why I want to show you how our process for getting things done has evolved over the years. Without firm operations in place, we would always be at the mercy of luck.

CHAPTER 9

OPERATIONS

Many people have been indoctrinated into the "work hard" way of doing things. That sounds like a good thing at the outset, but there is an ugly side. In reality, just working hard is not enough.

Here's a little secret: if you feel like you are working *too* hard at something, you probably could find an easier way to do the same thing. This is where instituting real operations helps, because it puts everyone on the same page of working smarter, not harder. Keep track of your processes with clear documentation, so mistakes aren't repeated and there is a standard approach to any given task. Think about it as creating an ongoing company ledger.

THE COMMUNICATIONS AND OPERATIONS OF A COMPANY ARE THE SAME AS THE HEART TO YOUR BODY

You and your team could be considered the brain of your company, enabling the cohesive logic and decision-making that keeps everyone on the same page. But it is the clearly defined roles each team member plays that create the heartbeat. Without a company process, logic can easily get confused or obscured by emotions and short-term thinking. There is no cohesion, and then you have a Subtle on your hands.

Clearly define who's doing what—no one should feel like they don't know what they're doing on any given day. These records all go into the company ledger.

All of the improvements we've made to our operations over the years have been based on real-world lessons we've learned. Every mistake we have made has turned into a lesson that we have recorded in the company ledger. These mistakes have improved our performance because they revealed to us things we didn't know about ourselves. As a result, we've become more self-aware as a company.

Failures at the scale we made three years ago would never happen today—that's why we can work with larger clients, take on hundreds of thousands of dollars' worth of work, and push our own boundaries to continue growing as a company. The failures in our early operations helped us to neatly hone the process we follow today, after ten years of experience in this game.

Our team has gotten a lot better at communicating with one another, and part of that is thanks to technological improvements. But the other reason is the soul of the team coming together—the team I have today is more compatible with one another than ever before.

Communication is a challenge we've had to wrestle with since the very beginning. For a lot of our company's history, we've had an irregular heartbeat. This was mostly because we work remotely as a team. Years ago, the team did all of their communications through Skype, TeamSpeak, and email. Today, we have even more tools at our disposal: Slack, iMessage, Google Hangouts/Meeting, Google Drive, InVision, TestFlight, Asana, TeamGantt, Adobe Creative Cloud. Technology not only allows us to communicate more efficiently, but it's also had a really beneficial effect on our clients.

But I cannot emphasize enough how technology cannot serve as a substitute for the spirit the heart needs to keep running. A passive-aggressive boss is still going to be passive-aggressive over Slack. Slack is a system for communication. Therefore, the systems we set up are not replacements for our personal interactions. That's why I make sure that everyone gets together at least a few times per year. This is what builds the spirit of the heart and encourages people to define their roles at Chop Dawg. Why? Because these get-togethers allow people with different skills to hang out. A marketer can become friends with a developer and they can expand their skill-sets together.

We aren't hamstrung to any single location, which is great, but I don't want us to be isolated from one another either. So, as I'm expanding Chop Dawg, I've been setting up clusters of team members in several major cities, such as Atlanta and Seattle. While we'll always be distributed across the country, I do like the idea of some of our team members getting close and being able to work with one another. This gets the creative juices flowing.

There is value in a mix of digital and in-person communication because it keeps the spirit going while the technology keeps the efficiency going. I'd like to go through the evolution of how Chop Dawg has handled operations over time. As you'll see through my self-analysis of our operations, had we kept the same operations as we had in our early years, we would not be here today. Not even close.

FROM 2009 TO 2011, WE WERE ALL DISORGANIZED. WE HAD NO PROCESS

Every conversation between a client and the early Chop Dawg team would be handled over email or phone.

Life is just so much easier when you know where to find everything. We made it very difficult on ourselves to reference things later, because we didn't keep any organized records. We felt like total messes.

As for the contracts that our clients signed, we had no legal counsel or expertise in drawing them up—we just used a basic template. As a result, the contracts barely protected us from anything. And because we only required full payment upon completion of projects, this led to our being occasionally stiffed on the bill after completion of services rendered.

Our approach from this era sprouted from two key failures:

1. Clients could take forever to give feedback, making jobs drag on for months, yet we were still paid the same flat rate for our service.
2. Our contracts didn't lock in approved designs—we couldn't prevent them from requesting design changes even after months of code. This doubled (and occasionally tripled) our work, while our revenue stayed at the same set rate.

FROM 2011 TO 2013, WE BEGAN FLESHING OUT OUR CONTRACTS TO DOCUMENT OUR PROCESS, AND BEGAN HOLDING CLIENTS MORE ACCOUNTABLE

For instance, we used to lure clients with an unlimited maintenance window; however, if a client's website broke down or they wanted us to add something a year after the project, we would be responsible *forever*, without any additional pay. That obviously was not sustainable.

Our new contracts included a specific time limit on website maintenance. Where we used to require no initial payment up front, we began asking for an initial payment of 25 percent. This helped us weed through those who didn't have sufficient funding for their projects and ensured that our clients were more serious, as they had money on the line.

We also used better tools for communications—Skype let us know when any of us were online, and TeamSpeak worked for quick conversations. As a result, internal communications improved drastically from the previous years of playing phone tag and waiting on emails. Before, team members didn't have a place to communicate with me when they were stuck with a client or needed assistance. So we instituted weekly check-ins so we could update each other about client work all at once.

Finally, we wrote up our first formal proposals for clients, which documented everything they should expect to receive from us and when. This really improved how we set expectations for ourselves as well as for the clients. I cannot emphasize enough how much our headaches decreased by adding provisions to organize our efforts and cover our butts in the proposal.

Better contracts held clients more accountable and held us more accountable as well. More projects were brought to the finish line on time and on budget.

Even with all those improvements to our contracts, we weren't without our troubles:

1. There was still too much wiggle room for clients to exploit the contract and cause delays.
2. Skype at that time still had terrible connections, even on decent internet speeds. Also, if more than one person wanted to join, they'd have to accept the call at the first ring to get everyone in, or you'd have to restart. With TeamSpeak, team members were always logged on, meaning that your computer was a 24/7 microphone; but to the team, it felt more like a Big Brother than a communication tool.
3. Uploading all mock-ups to our servers worked for the team, but this setup confused clients—they now had to browse server directories to view their files, versus just opening an email with an attachment.

4. Because our projects were growing larger, even a 25 percent up-front fee wasn't always enough. For some projects, we would go months without pay. In addition, clients still were still able to drag out projects using the limited margins our contracts gave them.

IN 2013 AND 2014, WE CONTINUED TO IMPROVE OUR PROPOSALS

This was all the more necessary once we made the transition from building small websites to large-scale apps. Before, we would work with many clients at once, but now we were working with just a few at a time. That brought in cash-flow issues that we didn't have to worry about before. To address the cash-flow problem, we handled payments on a monthly scale for the first time.

The cloud revolution was really beginning to kick off, so we took advantage of it by using Dropbox for organized storage of designs and files. This proved to be a much more intuitive option for clients, too, versus having to look through server directories.

Still, our operations were not without their faults.

1. Skype was still difficult for clients to use, especially when you had sometimes four to eight people joining one call per week. (This would change in late 2013, when Google Hangouts changed the game.)

2. We learned within the first year that things can still change in mock-ups, even *if* wireframes are approved first. Sometimes we still scrapped months of work at the client's request, forcing us to restart and waste thousands of dollars in labor and time.

3. We still didn't have that silver bullet to guard against some clients taking advantage of us. When clients asked for things outside the scope of the proposal, we would usually say OK in order to provide "the best customer service." But for every inch we gave, some clients would take miles from us, derailing projects and timelines, and then putting the blame and responsibility on us for missing targeted dates and expectations.

4. While Dropbox was a good solution, it was expensive and it still didn't fix the issue with receiving organized client feedback.

5. Having weekly meetings started eating up everyone's time and interfering with the work we needed to get done.

FROM 2014 TO 2016, WE STARTED TO MOVE TOWARD THE WAY WE OPERATE TODAY

We moved from sharing designs on Dropbox to Google Drive, which offered a better experience for much less money.

It also gave us our holy grail for moving projects along

smoothly: clients could make comments on each individual design to keep things organized.

We also set boundaries to our weekly meetings, so we could get work done on time, while keeping our team sane. There was still communication throughout the week, but the team could focus on the things clients cared about the most, such as the actual work getting done.

To address the problem of trying to shoot a moving target, we didn't begin programming until *all* designs were done. Before our operations had been mixed, and now design and development were separated.

We moved away from our in-house solutions for team communications (which we weren't keeping up to date anymore) to HipChat—the precursor to Slack in the instant-messaging space. (Sidenote: HipChat was actually just acquired by Slack in early 2018.) We also educated new clients that anything they requested outside the proposal would add more time and costs. This made us go from looking like the bad guys to looking like saviors by addressing this sooner rather than later. It's much like remodeling your home. You wouldn't start taking down walls and making major decisions before fully planning the scope of work and knowing its associated costs, as this can negatively impact your budget. It's important to know the full scope of work before getting started.

As you probably expect by now, more problems still emerged even with our solutions in place. Customer expectations were increasing, and this was the deeper issue that our company would need to address:

1. Even though programming was totally based on approved designs, we still had some big errors and misunderstandings where the functionality did not fit the desired design. One of our clients called me one day, furious about how his app was conveying unread messages. The error was based on one small, overlooked detail—was the total number of unread messages determined by message threads or individual messages themselves? This wasn't addressed in the design phase, when it should have been. We needed to figure out how to further intertwine design and programming. Separating these operations was not enough.

2. Our project lengths had grown from a few months of work to an average of six to twelve months. We should have kept extensive documentation on how we managed these big projects; that would have made us faster and better at our jobs when new work came in. Not having this documentation caused frustrations for the clients and added time and work for us.

3. Our proposals, which we offered for free, had become incredibly detailed (usually more than fifty pages) and took us a few weeks to write. We often had ten to

twenty prospective clients a month asking for proposals, yet only a handful would prove to be serious about working with us. This wasted a lot of time, especially because I was personally writing the proposals. This was hundreds of hours lost. I was losing us thousands of dollars each month in opportunity costs.

4. As we continued to grow, we needed more team members. But as our operations matured, so did the learning curve for onboarding new team members because things were more complicated. It took longer to get up to speed with our culture, what we do, and how we do it.

FROM 2016 TO 2018, WE CAME UP WITH SOME IMPORTANT CONCEPTS TO INTRODUCE TO OUR OPERATIONS

Before, we had treated design as only a form and not as a function. But the harsh reality we realized was that design is not just how pretty something looks. It also determines how the entire user experience feels.

Introducing product flows served as blueprints to the clients. They could see how their products could look good and *feel* good from the start. This new process added only an extra week of design, while protecting us from the risk of adding months in programming in case there was an error, like with the message notification situation. These product flows gave everyone—developers, designers, and clients—a much clearer picture and sense of direction. The only back-and-forth now needed was bug testing and populating content at the end of coding.

We also introduced a letter of intent (LOI) that we required all potential clients to sign before we would create a proposal. This LOI acknowledged that our proposals would expire if the client did not move forward with us within twenty-eight days (four weeks). Clients had the option of paying a refundable deposit of 20 percent of the project costs to keep it open once twenty-eight days had passed. If they chose not to, and the proposal expired, our services would become inaccessible for one full calendar year. This change scared away everyone who wasn't serious about working with us. Our time writing proposals was cut down by more than half, yet we kept the same amount of work happening. Furthermore, I brought some of the team into the proposal-writing process, and it was no longer just me.

We also began instating a noncompete clause for all of our active clients, ensuring that they could trust that we weren't working on their projects and their competitors' projects at the same time.

We switched from Google Drive to InVision for organizing all designs and documentation, which also allowed us, for the first time, to start designing nonfunctional prototypes (NFPs) to help our clients raise capital. The

NFP also ushered in a new opportunity for us to create a new entry-level service, which brought in more client volume. Some of these NFP clients have become full-scale clients. By adding the NFP as a service, clients could not only continue to give us feedback in real time on designs, but it also gave us the ability to bypass the programming process to give live demos.

We utilized email in a new way by sending recaps after every meeting to serve as a clear paper trail of all conversations. One of the mantras I have picked up in my entrepreneurial career is "cover your ass."

I had been mostly acting as the de facto project manager for all work, and this was becoming very overwhelming and time-consuming, when, in reality, I needed to be focusing on the bigger picture for Chop Dawg. I brought on some project managers and a chief operating officer who not only helped manage clients so that the rest of the team could focus on work but also instituted better hiring and onboarding practices to get our team up to speed more quickly.

AS YOU CAN SEE, THE PROCESS OF BUILDING OUT YOUR OPERATIONS IS SOMETHING THAT TAKES TIME

I'll never stop tinkering with the Chop Dawg formula to improve on it. We'll always come up with new ways to bring the team and clients closer together. It's a life of constantly overhauling things while maintaining the parts that work.

One of my favorite baseball players growing up was Roy "Doc" Halladay, who was perhaps the most dominant pitcher in baseball from 2002 to 2011. The day he was traded to my Philadelphia Phillies was perhaps the peak of my teenage years.

What made Roy Halladay so great was that he wasn't always so flawless. In fact, the start of his professional career was a mess. Although he played reasonably well in the rookie season, the following year it was as if he had forgotten how to pitch. He ended up being cut from the major leagues and sent back to the minors.

For most baseball players, this would have spelled the end of their careers. Most would have quit then and there. Not Roy Halladay, though. He used the struggle to reinvent his pitching game from the ground up. When he started his career, he had come up with an overhand four-seam fastball and curveball. In the minors, he dropped his arm slot and started throwing a two-seamer. With the help of mentors and others, he learned how to throw a perfect cutter. He discovered, studied, and obsessed over the details, treating it as an art form, painting the corners with movement while maintaining the velocity to induce swing-and-misses that pitchers strive for. Roy Halladay used his failures to create a new process, improve himself, and ultimately become one of the greatest pitchers of a generation. There was nothing better than spending an evening down in South Philly, watching the doctor go to work on the opposing batting lineup.

You can never become complacent in how you do things or fall in love with the same routines just because they work for now. You must have the mindset of always asking yourself how you can improve, remembering that obstacles are a window to new opportunities. And the more you work on these improvements as a team rather than individualistically, the better.

THINK BACK TO CHAPTER 6 ON LEADERSHIP—A TEAM THRIVES ON MORE THAN THE WORK OF ITS STAR PLAYER

In 2018, Villanova won their third National Championship in the NCAA College Basketball tournament. Their lead scorer in the championship game was not their starter but one of their bench players named Donte DiVincenzo. He came in from the bench when his team was slumping and not only helped keep up the pace for the rest of his teammates by thirty-one points but also secured the team's victory and their place in NCAA history.

During the live broadcast of the game, one of the lead commentators observed that Villanova's recipe for dominating over the entire tournament was that their go-to guy was the open man on the court. It wasn't a single player; it wasn't a superstar; it was a full-team effort. You've heard the saying that you're as strong as your weakest link. This is the perfect example.

So many companies on the verge of becoming remarkable fall short due to the fact that they depend on one superstar instead of building a team of all-stars. There should be no singular "go-to" in your business; instead, there should be a collective of talent and expertise. The operation should not collapse if someone has to leave. That means that you haven't really set up your sustainable operations if your business is at that kind of risk.

TO ME, THE MOST POWERFUL WORD IN THE ENGLISH DICTIONARY IS "UNTIL"

Teach this word to every one of your team members and ingrain this word in your company's DNA.

You will not stop working until _____.

You will not stop fighting until _____.

You will not give in until _____.

You will continue to push one another until _____.

"Until" is the objective that you set out to accomplish in everything you do, no matter how small or large. It means you must do what is necessary until it gets done. So ask yourself, with your company, with yourself, how many objectives are you working on until you accomplish what you need to?

If you want your company to make $10,000 a month in recurring revenue, you can't simply tell your team that's what you want. It's your responsibility as a leader to lay out the road map for your team for getting there, no matter how much time it takes.

"Until" is the most powerful word in the English language, and we often fail to use it to our advantage.

Everything you do with your company must have a purpose behind it. Instead of doing too many things, focus on the few things that actually matter and keep working on those things until you accomplish what you set out to do. There is a saying that teams all aligned on the same mission can move mountains. But getting a team together means being clear about the objective and the role that each person plays. Everyone on the team should start the day knowing what they are doing to get to until.

I told myself back when we had thrown in the towel with Subtle that I was going to do everything I could until

I never felt disgusted with myself again. Setting up our ever-evolving operations has been therapeutic for me in the long run. I feel like now we have the framework as a team to get to until. I feel that with the positive evolution that we've had over the years with our operations, we are getting to the point that we will someday move mountains together.

CHAPTER 10

PURPOSE

I'm sure you've heard the sage advice "Find your passion" before.

It's preached in nearly every self-help exercise out there; it's taught to children in elementary school; it's in slogans geared toward entrepreneurs; it's encouraged by serial entrepreneurs and keynote motivational speakers, on podcasts, in YouTube videos, and in books.

Hell, in this book, I've been pretty much beating you over the head that you shouldn't start a business based on artificial goals such as wanting to make money or get acquired. You should only start a business with cause, with conviction, and really do it for something you truly believe in.

That is what separates those who succeed the majority of the time from those who fail and flame out.

THE PROBLEM WITH JUST "FINDING YOUR PASSION"

Passion should be something that pushes you, moves you, and motivates you. But passion alone can't do anything productive for you; think of it more as a cluster of energy. While you need that cluster of energy, passions alone aren't sustainable, because they can really change over time. One of the things I was first passionate about in my life were roller coasters. If you asked me at fifteen years old, I would have sworn to you my purpose in life was to be a roller coaster designer at Intamin or Bolliger & Mabillard (Rocky Mountain Coasters didn't exist then, or I'd be listing them, too). But clearly, this wasn't a book about roller coasters.

I turned that passion into finding my next passion, which was making my own websites.

Passions can evolve; they can also become dormant, just to be reinvigorated at a later date. You should be mindful of the link that ties your past passions together and what's fueling your passions now.

How do your passions connect and relate? Do they connect and relate to each other at all?

As you examine your passions, observe how they circle around a common theme.

I had to connect these dots in order to find my purpose. And let's remember that I would never have found my purpose if I had planned out my life's work when I was ten years old. Only through hindsight, and the years of experience and of knowing myself, have I been able to look back and determine my purpose.

Sabrina Mutukisna was the program manager for the California Teacher Pathway, which works with the community college system to train high school students to become teachers. Working in education did give her fulfillment. And Sabrina found that the students who had the fewest barriers to finding employment were those who felt best in the classroom. She also realized that grant-funded nonprofits were not a sustainable model for bringing in money year after year. By her last year working for the California Teacher Pathway, the nonprofit had a third of its budget, compared to when she had started. This would never be scalable, which she found frustrating.

At the same time, Sabrina had started her own cupcake business on the side. Working in the food service industry fueled her passion for building a local food system. She started thinking about how she could create a for-profit company that worked in both youth development and education. So Sabrina created the Town Kitchen, a community-driven food company that employs and empowers low-income youth to prepare and deliver food to corporate clients in Oakland and San Francisco. All box lunches that are made for the corporate clients are chef-prepared using ingredients sourced from local growers, producers, and food entrepreneurs.

The Town Kitchen has now become a regional jobs engine. By learning food preparation skills from highly regarded professional chefs, they have a path to getting into the food industry themselves. Meanwhile, corporations are able to put dollars into this community by becoming customers themselves, as the Town Kitchen caters a lot of their meetings and functions. It is also great for people already in the food industry, who can now be connected to the network to sell their ingredients.

By combining her passions for providing young people with fair-wage employment and entrepreneurial training and empowering an existing local food system, Sabrina discovered that her purpose was to create more equitable cities where young people are encouraged to stay and contribute.

WHEN FIGURING OUT YOUR PURPOSE, JUST THINK ABOUT HOW WE ARE PROBABLY LIVING IN ONE OF THE BIGGEST TURNING POINTS OF ALL TIME

I believe that we are on a teetering point where technology will grant us the opportunity to help generations of people and improve humanity. Technology could also wipe humanity off the face of the earth (but the optimist in me says that won't happen). Armed with all this potential, a lot of early entrepreneurs are passionate about solving all sorts of problems but haven't found a purpose to go with it.

But while entrepreneurship, at its core, is based on the problem-solution structure, there's an inherent limitation to it.

John Gavigan (the COO of SomaDetect and former CEO of 43North) brought this up to me before I'd even written this book:

"Doesn't that question [what problem are you trying to solve?] seem antiquated? We can't begin to solve problems right now that we don't even know exist."

He's right. The world will be quite different just five years after I release this book; it's hard to imagine what it'll be like in ten or twenty years. We don't know what the long-term effects will be for technologies that are just getting started. John brought up the case of augmented and virtual reality—we are getting to something that will allow people to navigate a more and more real-seeming virtual environment.

"Imagine the disruptions! Think of real estate. If I can have a meeting where real architects and interior designers create a virtual world to interact in, why would I ever need to rent space?"

Because the pace of technology is accelerating so much, John added:

"We need to forecast these potential challenges now, because look at the transition away from manufacturing in America. It destroyed America's cities. Cities were left to die because there was no plan."

AI has so many unknowns that it is hard to not find it absolutely captivating; however, it is hazy to accurately forecast what is going to happen. Imagine the new industries that have no rules written yet. Even though rewriting the rules is exciting, *a lot* of people will get lost in the shuffle. That makes purpose a little hazier to figure out, too. Or does it?

My purpose is to help the people who have great ideas, who don't have the technological resources, skills, or labor to bring them to reality. On top of it all, I want to have fun doing these things. This is why I run a technology agency that builds apps and software for others.

Technology agencies are incredibly hard to run and don't seem fun to run at the outset. Look at the marketplace in 2018—everyone wants to run the software, automate tasks, build things that solve problems at scale. The labor side isn't what people want to do, nor does it interest investors. Running an agency just isn't "sexy" to most aspiring entrepreneurs.

The thing is, I've found that our clients are actually much better at coming up with problem-solving ideas than I am. So by running an agency, I can assist those people who need it. Not everyone needs to be the direct problem solver; a lot of those people need help. This isn't the life for everyone, though. It takes a lot out of you, more than a standard business. It can get stressful, you're always on call, and you're the one where the buck stops. There is a lot of responsibility and grinding expected in an agency life that many, even some of the best entrepreneurs I have met, aren't cut out for.

But because I'm living in compatibility with my purpose, everything that I do has a point. So stress is different for me, because even when I'm experiencing stress, I still have that underlying feeling that life has a point. Even if I have to do something I don't enjoy at the moment, I can embrace it as part of my purpose.

YOU AREN'T BORN WITH YOUR PURPOSE

Purpose is the result of your upbringing, your beliefs, your environment, and the initial things you fall in love with doing. It's the result of a lot of different things, and it can pull you like an unseen magnet. Purpose isn't something that you can really plan.

That's why when others ask me how to find their purpose, I encourage them to identify their passions first. To me, finding your passion is the starting point of a giant road map for a journey that may take you only a few years or an entire lifetime to discover what drives you in life.

When I was in my early teens, I spent nearly every summer weekend visiting Six Flags Great Adventure in Jackson, New Jersey. It was my home away from home. Similar to that feeling you get when you walk through the rooms and halls of your childhood home, I still get the same feeling today when I venture through this little theme park located dead center in New Jersey. I love taking in the smell of the Pine Barrens and amusement park food, the surrounding buildings and colorful paint palette. I'm even soothed by the background music, the noises of the roller coasters, the sound of fountains, and the people all around. Great Adventure was where I discovered myself. I used it as a playground to study and soak in everything that was roller coasters and rides. By the time I was ten years old, having learned enough on the computer that I could make my own websites, I created a website called Great Adventure Online.

I BEGAN GREAT ADVENTURE ONLINE FOR ONLY ONE REASON: TO ENTERTAIN MYSELF

I wanted a place to test the skills that I'd built over the first decade or so of my life, while expressing my passion for all things Great Adventure. What I didn't realize yet was that others shared the same sentiment. But by the time I turned thirteen, my little website, Great Adventure Online, was ranked number one on Google—I was surpassing Six Flags' own website. Clearly, others shared the same sentiment, and my website had hundreds of thousands of visitors every month and thousands of registered users interacting with one another on message boards.

People flocked to my website to talk about the same things I wanted to talk about, share their memories, meet like-minded people, learn how to get the best deals, and so on. I was in heaven. I couldn't wait to wake up every morning and work on this website.

I felt like I had created something so much larger than myself. I had dozens of individuals asking to volunteer for the cause of connecting Great Adventure fans who wanted to share their expertise on the park. I began imagining what new features I could code next for the site.

And then, the mother lode of my childhood dreams came true: Six Flags itself actually wanted to work with me. It really didn't feel like anything could get more exciting than that. I forged a relationship with the park president, the head of public relations, marketing, and customer service. They began giving me the inside scoop of everything they were doing and planning; they invited me to significant media press releases and gave me behind-the-scenes tours to document and share with others.

My little theme park fan site grew so large that every time I made an appearance at Great Adventure, people knew who I was—not just theme park employees or executives but also regular park guests who were users and members of the website. Six Flags provided me with skip-the-line passes, complimentary food, everything you could think of.

Even as a teenager, all the praise and perks weren't what really mattered to me. What really mattered was feeling like I had the ability to build whatever I wanted and have real people use it. I loved that feeling so much. Waking up with a sense of pride, inspiration, motivation, and wonder is something I wish more people could experience.

I was an entrepreneur then without knowing it. I accidentally stumbled into it because it was what I wanted to do and what I was good at. Even though I didn't know what being an entrepreneur was then, I did know that I wanted to make an impact.

WHAT MAKES PURPOSE REMARKABLE IS THAT YOU REALLY DON'T KNOW HOW IT FEELS UNTIL IT FINALLY HITS YOU

Marci Harris is the CEO and cofounder of PopVox, an online platform that connects voters with lawmakers. As a former congressional staffer focusing on issues of health-care reform, Medicare, waste fraud, and abuse, she noticed that while Congress received much input from the public, Congress often failed to organize that input efficiently enough to employ it constructively.

Her on-the-job experiences shaped her purpose: Marci felt the insatiable drive to promote truly organized citizen participation to keep Congress accountable.

Today, by filling PopVox with public information about bills introduced in Congress, she facilitates public partic-ipation in politics to pave the way for better government. Marci is at the forefront of the civic technology movement, but she knows that while technology has allowed PopVox an unprecedented opportunity, the true purpose goes way beyond the technology itself.

As she states in her 2012 TED Talk:

"The true power of PopVox is not its technology. It is in the voices of people sharing their personal stories with their elected representatives."[5]

That's why the only thing I can recommend for finding your purpose is action and observation. Just get out there and look for what really needs to be changed. Sometimes your purpose can be derived from your on-the-job experience.

UNDERSTAND HOW YOU SPEND YOUR TIME, AND GIVE MORE VALUE TO YOUR TIME

Even if you spend twenty minutes to service one of your passions, that extra twenty minutes a day can equal 121.66 hours in a year. That's more than five days committed to trying to *do* something you like! It might not seem like a lot day to day, but your time really does add up.

Let's look at it from a 2018 perspective. If you spend an average of two hours a day on social media, that is 730 hours a year. That is almost one calendar month of an entire year that you've spent on social media. Imagine if you spent that time finding your passion or pursuing your purpose instead.

Your exercise:

---

5   "People and Technology Can Beat the Lobbyists,"_Marci Harris at TEDxMidAtlantic

I want you to really think about what you do with your time. Divorce yourself from thinking about what you want your purpose to be; instead, focus on just one thing:

What is the point of your living tomorrow? And how will you fulfill that? Fill in your response:

_____

_____

How do you feel about your response? Fill in your response:

_____

_____

What can you do to ensure you have a purpose tomorrow? Fill in your response:

_____

_____

Don't always think about the macro; just think about what would make you feel like you are living a little more purposefully each day. Don't always worry about how your week, your month, or even your year is going. Start with your day. This could be making it a goal to stop working every few hours, sit back, and soak in the day.

If I were running a company that I felt no purpose or connection to, I'd grow tired, be too stressed, and would most definitely quit. I feel purposeful in my work because everything that I do feels like it is a part of my DNA. Of course, it doesn't mean I don't have bad days. But it makes those days much easier when you know there is a point to everything that you're doing.

THAT IS WHY THOSE WHO DISCOVER THEIR PURPOSE STAY IN THE GAME MORE OFTEN THAN NOT FOR LIFE

One of my favorite examples of purpose is Kobe Bryant. (Yes, another basketball reference—what else would you expect from this book at this point?) The moment Kobe won his first championship, the ultimate destination in any NBA athlete's trajectory, you'd assume that he would feel that he had accomplished his purpose. But the following morning, Kobe was back in the gym, lifting weights, working on cardio, and practicing his shot to get ready for the next season. His purpose in life wasn't to win the Larry O'Brien Championship Trophy; it was to be the best basketball player ever to play the game.

That is what purpose does. It drives you beyond a monetary goal, a certain number of stores opened, or number of downloads of an app. Fulfillment isn't just about getting to a destination—it becomes about aligning your day-to-day activities with your purpose. You don't have short-term results in mind. You don't sacrifice little details and quality. You grow to love the grind and the journey and embrace every challenge and obstacle thrown at you. Your focus is on trying to quench that never-ending thirst to become the most impactful entrepreneur you can be.

I believe that purpose gives you a bit of a chip on your shoulder. Once you're clear and honest to yourself about what you want to accomplish in life and open about it with others, you set out to prove that, no matter the stakes. My sense of purpose has bred the competitor in me—"beating" others isn't *why* I do what I do, but that competitive instinct built into my purpose motivates me and shifts me into another gear.

However, purpose is ultimately selfless. It's not about you; it's about whether or not the purpose itself gets fulfilled, not if you are fulfilled. You don't care if it is your team that gets all of the credit; you just care that the purpose is honored and you achieve the desired results.

Sometimes things just don't operate at the pace that you expect and demand, but as long as you're becoming a little bit better every single day, you can feel fulfilled and excited for tomorrow.

EPILOGUE

I can't help looking back at my earliest days with such fondness. Those were the days when my entrepreneurial journey truly began, and I didn't even think of it as entrepreneurship at all. All I could think about was doing something that made me happy.

Years later, I've realized that feeling is the same one I chase today. I chase that feeling every day at Chop Dawg, when I am writing this book, when I speak to entrepreneurship classes at universities across the United States, and when I'm doing anything in between. It's the feeling that I can do whatever I set my mind to do. It took me years to come to the conclusion that I had actually discovered my life's purpose without realizing it when I was just thirteen years old.

Even more remarkable is that I don't recall a time in my life when I was more aligned with this very framework than when I was thirteen. That might sound preposterous, but this framework, when you really think about it, is all really built on common sense. I wasn't aware of it, though. Now that I am aware of the framework and have written it all out, it can finally serve as the compass I use every day to ensure I am staying on the right track. The framework will be the guide I need so I know I'm doing the right things for the right reasons.

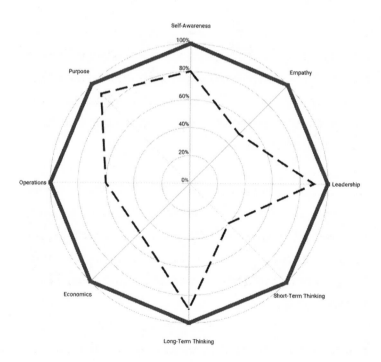

This is my personal framework, at the time that I write this:

- Self-awareness: 80 percent
- Empathy: 50 percent
- Leadership: 90 percent
- Short-term thinking: 40 percent
- Long-term thinking: 90 percent
- Economics: 50 percent
- Operations: 60 percent
- Purpose: 90 percent

The scores that I give myself on my personal framework are always changing. As I learn more about each principle, the score I have given myself is weighted differently. I am like a scientist; I score myself on the knowledge I have in that moment, but I do not believe for a second it is the perfect answer or, in this case, the perfect score. I hold myself accountable, and ask myself often, "Am I being truthful as I fill out this framework?"

The closer I am spiritually to being in lockstep with the framework, the closer I am to getting back the mindset I had when I was a teenager. The more I let greed, ego, and my own artificial desires overwhelm what really matters in entrepreneurship, the more those old feelings slip from my grasp.

It really is why I wrote this book. I want to remind myself

when times get tough, it is *that feeling* that makes it all
worth it.

THINK OF THE VERY FIRST EXAMPLE I PROVIDED YOU WAY BACK AT THE BEGINNING—THE BASKETBALL PLAYER

No one believes that if they can make a great free throw
or lay-up that they're destined to play in the NBA. Yet in
entrepreneurship, people believe that being able to sell
product, manage people, or create a website automatically
means that they are entrepreneurs. That just isn't the case.

Look at the best of the best basketball players in the world.
Just because they're great at all aspects of the game, understand the rules of the game, and have that natural talent
to play the game doesn't make them the best of the best.
Indeed, these are all critical components, but these talents
are moot without a genuine love of the game.

The best players in basketball are great because of their
obsession to do everything they can to be the best of the
best. It is their purpose in life, and they won't settle for
anything less.

This is the Entrepreneur's Framework in a nutshell. There
is no such thing as perfection. The way to leverage this
framework is to always look at where you stand in rela-
tion to all eight principles; identify where you are weakest,

to improve upon it; and identify how to continue to grow yourself overall.

You want to look back at yourself six months earlier and question why you thought the way you thought and acted the way you acted, because you now know so much more. I want to be embarrassed by my former self; when I reread this book a decade from now, I hope that I cringe because of how much more I know compared to now (and hopefully this forces me to create iterations of this book as I continue to learn on my own entrepreneurial journey).

You're not the best you can be right now, and that's great. What makes the framework magical is letting go of the fear of being wrong. The more you put into the framework, the more it gives back to you. The more it gives back to you, the more you want to add to it and teach it yourself.

My way might not work for you, and that's totally fine. As I've introduced this framework to other entrepreneurs, I've found that it works best as a starting point that you can customize for yourself. You need to work the framework into something that is compatible with your style and core values. My hope is that this framework keeps you focused on what is most important to you, helps you become mindful about your progress, and eliminates the noise and distractions that entrepreneurship will bring. Where too many people get caught up in the glory, this framework will encourage you to remain hungry, motivated, grounded, and inspired.

THIS IS A FOREVER LIVING, BREATHING FRAMEWORK (AND BOOK)

I am confident that my observations, beliefs, and fundamentals of this framework will alter. I've tried to make this book timeless, but that's an almost impossible task. No matter what, things change and things become dated. So if you want to challenge this framework, do it! Improve on it; add your own expertise, experience, and lessons that make it better for *everyone*. This framework is now as much yours as it is mine. In the New Economy, we're all part of a bigger machine pushing us ever toward being the most efficient, most productive, and most fulfilled possible.

It really is never too late to consider entrepreneurial thinking. Whether it leads you to entrepreneurship or something else equally exciting, I suggest that you really get into it. You have the capability to make change. Start by creating value for someone else—it can literally be just one person at first. I hope that one day I read about your good deeds.

If you embrace this framework, you've embraced being more than just an entrepreneur. You've embraced *becoming a student of entrepreneurship*—it's the recipe for being successful in this game, now and always.

ACKNOWLEDGMENTS

I've had the privilege of knowing so many great, influential people over the course of my life. I cannot express how grateful I am to them, and without these people, neither this book nor my entrepreneurial career would exist. I owe it all to them; they are why I get to do what I do. When I think about them or see them, they always remind me why I am so grateful for the good life I have been able to make for myself and, hopefully, others. To name a few of my long list: Kegan Gilbert, Michael Baker, Brian Jackson, Johnny Earle, Devin Olson, Ian Brennan, Kimberly DeMaggio, Carrie Williams, Brandon Teller, Eddie Contento, Matthew Kaiser, Michael Taylor, Lee Shlamowitz, Josue Castillo, Brad Aronson, Joseph Marrone, and to the extraordinary team we have at Chop Dawg, past, present, and future. Thank you all.

With that said, I would be doing a disservice without directly naming a few people. First and foremost, I must thank Mason Carter, my right-hand man throughout this entire book creation process. Without you, this book would not exist. You've in essence become the CEO of this book, the coauthor of this book, and head promoter of this book, all wrapped into one individual. I'm forever thankful for you and your friendship. Your name deserves to be on the front cover with me for everything you've done to make this book a reality.

Second, I must thank Tamerah Slaughter, without whom I would have given up on this book altogether. She is the voice that keeps telling me to keep going, keep working, and share this with the masses. And she's the voice that turned a pile of incoherent thoughts, ideas, and strategies into the book that you now read. You're the best partner in crime anyone could ever ask for and an even better mom to our four-legged children. I love you.

Third, a special thank-you to Joshua Winkles, who implanted the idea in me years ago that I had to write a book. Outside of the enormous debt I owe you for helping the entire team at Chop Dawg grow over the years, I also owe you a thank-you for being right by my side, being my counsel in times of hardship and stresses, pushing me, and making me into a better entrepreneur and, in this case, author. Many of the principles in this book are what you've instilled in me through the few years that we've now had the chance to work together.

Fourth, I must thank the dozens who graciously gave me their time to not only be interviewed for this book but also to make me a better entrepreneur, role model, and student of the game. I know how valuable all of your time is, and I am forever grateful for you helping me. Many who also helped provided me with remarkable insight into how to make this book even better and more impactful than anything I could have ever dreamed to achieve myself.

Lastly, I must thank my father. I couldn't have been any luckier growing up with someone who I not only considered a role model and inspiration; but my best friend. You instilled in me a work ethic, the philosophy to always look out and help others before yourself, how to roll with the punches and get up when others would have surely quit, and discover my purpose and calling in life. I couldn't have had a better upbringing, and I am grateful every day for you. I love you.

ABOUT THE AUTHOR

JOSHUA H. DAVIDSON

has been working since he was sixteen: first as an entrepreneur, then as a business advisor, writer, speaker, and most recently as a nationally-syndicated radio and podcast host. Today, he runs a full stack design and development team based throughout the entire United States that is a "Temporary CTO + App Development Team for Hire" for companies. To date, Joshua's company Chop Dawg has been the driving force behind more than two hundred new product launches and businesses. Joshua has been featured on NBC, MSNBC, CBS, FOX, AOL, *Forbes, Mashable, Inc. Magazine, Huffington Post* and *Startup Grind*, and has been named a Top 100 Marketing Influencer by Brand24 and Entrepreneur of the Year by *Philly Happening Magazine*.

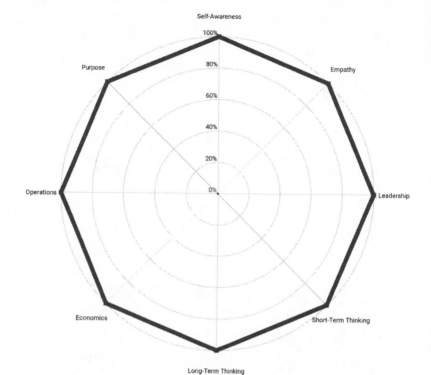

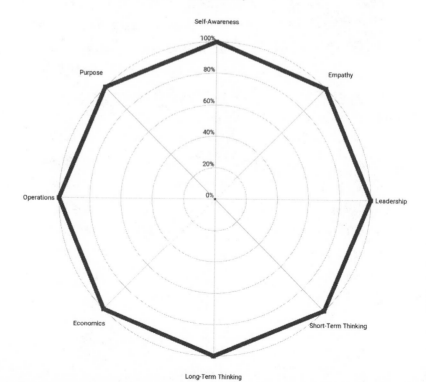

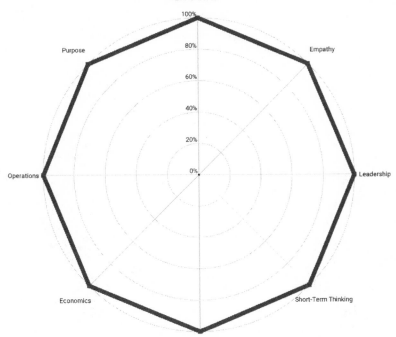

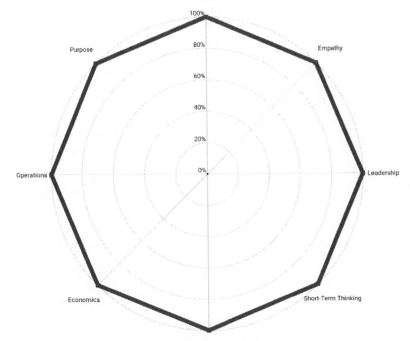

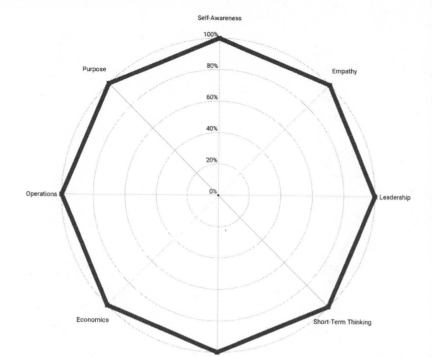

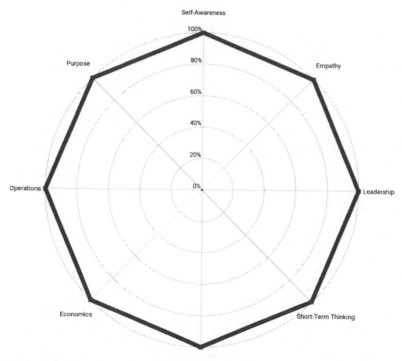

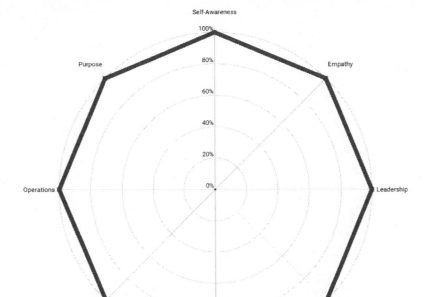

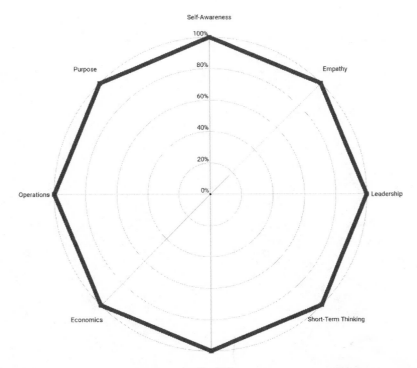

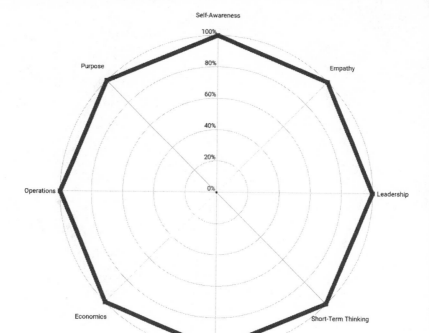

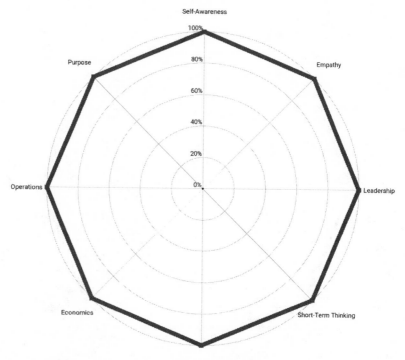

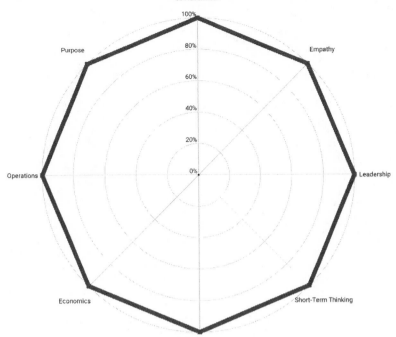

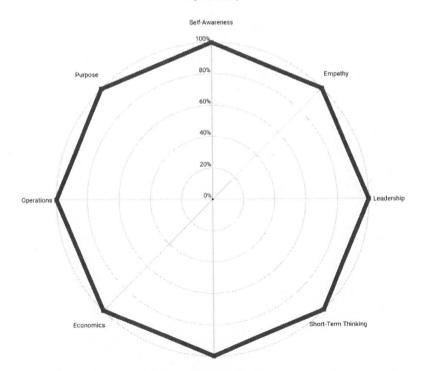

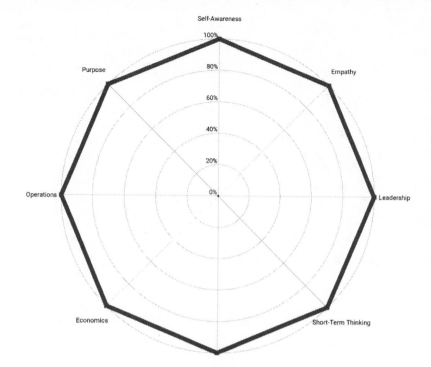

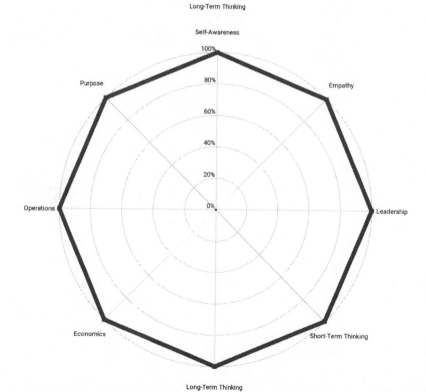

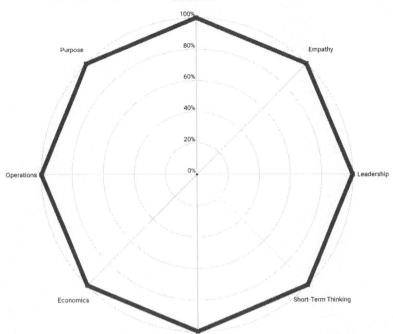

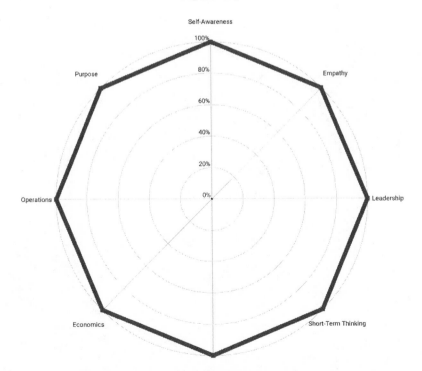

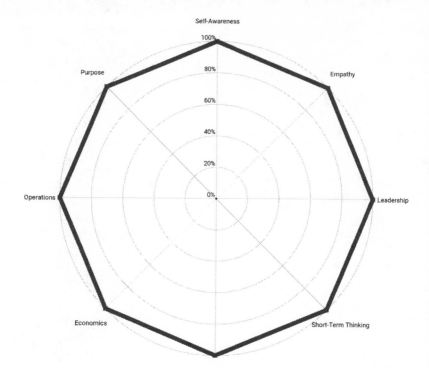

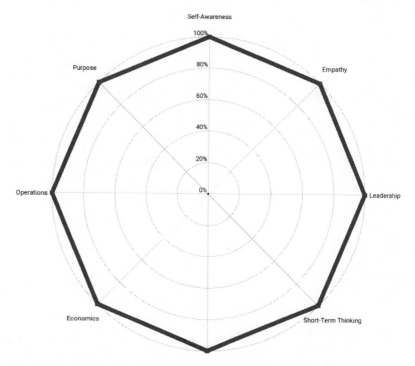

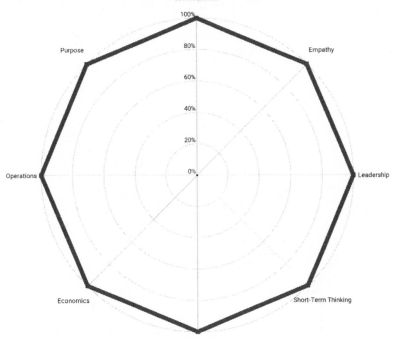

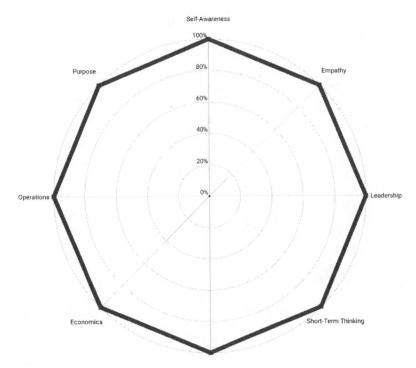

50375 00718

Made in the USA
San Bernardino, CA
21 November 2018